fiX *with a* ...K *desserts*

100
sensational sweets
made easy
with a mix

WILEY
Wiley Publishing, Inc.

Copyright © 2010 by General Mills, Minneapolis, Minnesota. All rights reserved.

Published by Wiley Publishing, Inc., Hoboken, New Jersey

Published simultaneously in Canada

No part of this publication may be reproduced, stored in a retrieval system, or transmitted in any form or by any means, electronic, mechanical, photocopying, recording, scanning, or otherwise, except as permitted under Section 107 or 108 of the 1976 United States Copyright Act, without either the prior written permission of the Publisher, or authorization through payment of the appropriate per-copy fee to the Copyright Clearance Center, Inc., 222 Rosewood Drive, Danvers, MA 01923, (978) 750-8400, fax (978) 750-4470, or on the web at www.copyright.com. Requests to the Publisher for permission should be addressed to the Permissions Department, John Wiley & Sons, Inc., 111 River Street, Hoboken, NJ 07030, (201) 748-6011, fax (201) 748-6008, or online at http://www.wiley.com/go/permissions.

Trademarks: Wiley and the Wiley Publishing logo are trademarks or registered trademarks of John Wiley & Sons and/or its affiliates. All other trademarks referred to herein are trademarks of General Mills. Wiley Publishing, Inc., is not associated with any product or vendor mentioned in this book.

Limit of Liability/Disclaimer of Warranty: While the publisher and author have used their best efforts in preparing this book, they make no representations or warranties with respect to the accuracy or completeness of the contents of this book and specifically disclaim any implied warranties of merchantability or fitness for a particular purpose. No warranty may be created or extended by sales representatives or written sales materials. The advice and strategies contained herein may not be suitable for your situation. You should consult with a professional where appropriate. Neither the publisher nor author shall be liable for any loss of profit or any other commercial damages, including but not limited to special, incidental, consequential, or other damages.

For general information on our other products and services or for technical support, please contact our Customer Care Department within the United States at (800) 762-2974, outside the United States at (317) 572-3993 or fax (317) 572-4002.

Wiley also publishes its books in a variety of electronic formats. Some content that appears in print may not be available in electronic books. For more information about Wiley products, visit our web site at www.wiley.com.

Library of Congress Cataloging-in-Publication Data

Betty Crocker fix with a mix desserts.
    p. cm.
Includes index.
ISBN 978-0-470-61799-1 (cloth/spiral-bound)
1. Desserts. 2. Brand name products. I. Title: Fix with a mix desserts.
TX773.B49287 2010
641.8'6—dc22
                    2009049269

Manufactured in China

10 9 8 7 6 5 4 3 2 1

Cover photo (clockwise from top): Chocolate Mousse–Raspberry Cake (page 42), Chai Latte Cupcakes (page 76), Chocolate Ganache Mini Cakes (page 22), Turtle Tassies (page 8), Apricot Petits Fours (page 20)

general mills

Editorial Director: Jeff Nowak

Publishing Manager: Christine Gray

Editor: Grace Wells

Recipe Development and Testing: Betty Crocker Kitchens

Photography: General Mills Photography Studios and Image Library

Photographer: Chuck Nields

Food Stylists: Amy Peterson and Suzanne Finley

Prop Stylist: Michele Joy

wiley publishing, inc.

Publisher: Natalie Chapman

Associate Publisher: Jessica Goodman

Executive Editor: Anne Ficklen

Editor: Adam Kowit

Production Editor: Abby Saul

Cover Design: Suzanne Sunwoo

Art Director: Tai Blanche

Interior Design and Layout: Holly Wittenberg

Manufacturing Manager: Kevin Watt

The Betty Crocker Kitchens seal guarantees success in your kitchen. Every recipe has been tested in America's Most Trusted Kitchens™ to meet our high standards of reliability, easy preparation and great taste.

Find more great ideas at *BettyCrocker*.com

dear friends,

There's nothing like a home-baked dessert to make any occasion special. And with *Betty Crocker Fix-with-a-Mix Desserts*, it's never been easier. Simply start out with your favorite Betty Crocker mix, add one or two simple ingredients, and—voila!—you have a fabulous dessert that tastes terrific and looks sensational.

What can you make with a mix? A lot more than you may have guessed! Start with cookie mix to whip up fabulously flavored cookies and bars like Chocolate-Marshmallow Pillows and Almond Streusel–Cherry Cheesecake Bars, or use it to create luscious fruit desserts like Southern Apple Crumble. Turn cake mix into decadent layer cakes like Chocolate Mousse–Raspberry Cake, adorable cupcakes, and even cheesecake! Bite-size desserts are more popular than ever, so don't miss the chapter of marvelous mini sweets to add a fun touch to any occasion. There's even a chapter of gluten-free sweets to sample.

So get ready for foolproof dessert recipes to be proud of. Whip up a delicious dessert today with an easy mix at your fingertips. No one will guess your secret ingredient!

happy baking!

Betty Crocker

page
12

page
58

page
82

contents

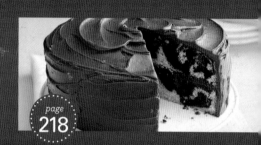

page 132

page 172

page 194

chapter one

page **8**

page **24**

page **22**

tiny desserts

turtle tassies

prep time: 1 hour   *start to finish:* 1 hour   [48 TASSIES]

1 pouch (1 lb 1.5 oz) Betty Crocker sugar cookie mix

Butter and egg called for on cookie mix pouch

2 bags (14 oz each) caramels, unwrapped

⅓ cup whipping cream

¾ cup dark chocolate chips

½ cup chopped pecans

1 Heat oven to 375°F. Lightly spray 48 mini muffin cups with cooking spray.

2 Make cookie dough as directed on pouch, using butter and egg. Shape dough into 48 (1-inch) balls. Press 1 ball into bottom of each muffin cup, pressing up sides to fill cups.

3 Bake 8 to 9 minutes or until edges begin to brown. Meanwhile, in 3-quart saucepan, heat caramels and whipping cream over medium heat, stirring frequently, until melted. Reduce heat to low.

4 Remove pans from oven; gently press end of wooden spoon handle into bottoms and against sides of cookie cups to flatten, being careful not to make holes in dough.

5 Bake 2 to 3 minutes longer or until edges are light golden brown. Immediately spoon ½ teaspoon (about 4) chocolate chips into each cookie cup.

6 Spoon about 1 tablespoon caramel mixture into each cookie cup. Immediately top with pecans. Cool 5 minutes; remove from pans with narrow spatula.

1 TASSIE: Calories 150; Total Fat 6g (Saturated Fat 2.5g; Trans Fat 0g); Cholesterol 15mg; Sodium 85mg; Total Carbohydrate 22g (Dietary Fiber 0g); Protein 1g EXCHANGES: ½ Starch, 1 Other Carbohydrate, 1 Fat CARBOHYDRATE CHOICES: 1½

sweet note These tiny tassies can be made ahead. Store them in an airtight container in the freezer for up to 1 month.

strawberry cheesecake bites

prep time: **15 minutes**   *start to finish:* **3 hours**   [32 CHEESECAKE BITES]

1 pouch (1 lb 1.5 oz) Betty Crocker sugar cookie mix

⅓ cup butter or margarine, melted

2 tablespoons all-purpose flour

3 eggs

2 packages (8 oz each) cream cheese, softened

¾ cup sugar

1 teaspoon vanilla

¾ cup strawberry spreadable fruit

1 Heat oven to 350°F. Spray bottom only of 13 × 9-inch pan with cooking spray.

2 In medium bowl, stir cookie mix, butter, flour and 1 of the eggs until soft dough forms. Press evenly in pan.

3 Bake 15 to 18 minutes or until light golden brown. Cool 15 minutes. Meanwhile, in large bowl, beat cream cheese, sugar, vanilla and remaining 2 eggs with electric mixer on medium speed until smooth. Spread evenly over crust in pan.

4 Place spreadable fruit in small resealable food-storage plastic bag; seal bag. Cut off tiny corner of bag. Squeeze spreadable fruit in 3 lines the length of the pan. Use knife to pull spread from side to side through cream cheese mixture at 1-inch intervals.

5 Bake 25 to 30 minutes longer or until filling is set. Refrigerate until chilled, about 2 hours.

6 For bars, cut into 8 rows by 4 rows. Store covered in refrigerator.

1 CHEESECAKE BITE: Calories 180; Total Fat 9g (Saturated Fat 5g; Trans Fat 1g); Cholesterol 40mg; Sodium 100mg; Total Carbohydrate 22g (Dietary Fiber 0g); Protein 2g EXCHANGES: ½ Starch, 1 Other Carbohydrate, 2 Fat CARBOHYDRATE CHOICES: 1½

sweet note To make extra tiny treats and add a new shape to your cookie tray, cut bars diagonally in half to make triangles.

double-chocolate caramel-coffee cups

prep time: 30 minutes *start to finish:* 1 hour 10 minutes [36 COOKIE CUPS]

cookie cups

1 teaspoon instant espresso coffee granules

1 tablespoon water

1 pouch (1 lb 1.5 oz) Betty Crocker double chocolate chunk cookie mix

3 tablespoons vegetable oil

1 egg

topping

1 container (1 lb) vanilla creamy ready-to-spread frosting

2 tablespoons caramel-flavored liqueur or cold coffee

½ cup marshmallow creme

2 tablespoons caramel topping

1 Heat oven to 375°F. Spray 36 mini muffin cups with cooking spray or line with mini paper baking cups.

2 In large bowl, dissolve espresso granules in water. Add cookie mix, oil and egg; stir until soft dough forms. Shape dough into 36 (1-inch) balls; place in muffin cups.

3 Bake 8 to 9 minutes or until set. With end of wooden spoon handle, immediately make indentation in center of each cookie to form a cup. Cool 30 minutes. Remove from pan.

4 In small bowl, stir frosting and liqueur until well blended. Gently stir in marshmallow creme. Spoon frosting mixture evenly into each cookie cup. Store covered in refrigerator. Before serving, use fork to drizzle each cookie cup with caramel topping.

1 COOKIE CUP: Calories 130; Total Fat 5g (Saturated Fat 1.5g; Trans Fat 1g); Cholesterol 5mg; Sodium 85mg; Total Carbohydrate 20g (Dietary Fiber 0g); Protein 0g EXCHANGES: 1½ Other Carbohydrate, 1 Fat CARBOHYDRATE CHOICES: 1

sweet note If you have only one 12-cup mini muffin pan, cover the extra dough to keep it from drying out. Bake one pan at a time, cooling the pan completely before refilling with dough.

lemon dream cups

prep time: 40 minutes   *start to finish:* 2 hours 10 minutes   [36 COOKIE CUPS]

1 pouch (1 lb 1.5 oz) Betty Crocker sugar cookie mix

½ cup whole almonds, ground

6 tablespoons butter or margarine, melted

1 package (3 oz) cream cheese, softened

1 jar (12 oz) lemon curd

⅔ cup fluffy white whipped ready-to-spread frosting (from 12-oz container)

½ cup frozen (thawed) whipped topping

1 teaspoon grated lemon peel

2 tablespoons sliced almonds

1 Heat oven to 375°F. Spray 36 mini muffin cups with cooking spray.

2 In large bowl, stir cookie mix, ground almonds, butter and cream cheese until soft dough forms. Shape dough into 36 (1¼-inch) balls. Press 1 ball in bottom and up side of each muffin cup.

3 Bake 12 to 15 minutes or until golden brown. Cool completely in pan, about 30 minutes.

4 Remove cookie cups from pan. Fill each with about 1½ teaspoons lemon curd.

5 In small bowl, mix frosting and whipped topping until well blended. Pipe or spoon 1 rounded teaspoon frosting mixture on top of each filled cookie cup. Garnish with lemon peel and sliced almonds. Store covered in refrigerator.

1 COOKIE CUP: Calories 140; Total Fat 6g (Saturated Fat 2.5g; Trans Fat 1g); Cholesterol 15mg; Sodium 65mg; Total Carbohydrate 21g (Dietary Fiber 0g); Protein 1g EXCHANGES: 1½ Other Carbohydrate, 1 Fat CARBOHYDRATE CHOICES: 1½

sweet note Look for jars of lemon curd near the jams and jellies at the grocery store. For a fun flavor switch, make a few cupcakes with lime curd and top with grated lime peel.

mini candy bar cupcakes

prep time: **20 minutes** *start to finish:* **1 hour 10 minutes** [72 MINI CUPCAKES]

5 bars (2.1 oz each) chocolate-covered crispy peanut-buttery candy

1 box Betty Crocker SuperMoist® white cake mix

1¼ cups water

⅓ cup vegetable oil

3 egg whites

1 container (12 oz) milk chocolate whipped ready-to-spread frosting

sweet note Bake these adorable cupcakes ahead of time but don't frost. Freeze in an airtight container, then frost and decorate after removing them from the freezer.

1 Heat oven to 350°F (325°F for dark or nonstick pans). Place mini paper baking cup in each of 72 mini muffin cups. Finely chop enough candy to equal ¾ cup (about 2 bars).

2 In large bowl, beat cake mix, water, oil and egg whites with electric mixer on low speed 30 seconds. Beat on medium speed 2 minutes, scraping bowl occasionally. Beat in chopped candy on low speed just until blended. Divide batter evenly among muffin cups (about ⅔ full). Refrigerate any remaining cake batter until ready to use.

3 Bake 12 to 16 minutes or until toothpick inserted in center comes out clean. Cool 5 minutes; remove from pan to cooling rack. Cool completely, about 30 minutes. Frost cupcakes with frosting. Coarsely chop remaining candy. Place candy pieces on frosting, pressing down slightly. Store cupcakes loosely covered at room temperature.

1 MINI CUPCAKE: Calories 80; Total Fat 3.5g (Saturated Fat 1.5g, Trans Fat 0.5g); Cholesterol 0mg; Sodium 65mg; Total Carbohydrate 11g (Dietary Fiber 0g); Protein 0g EXCHANGES: 1 Other Carbohydrate, ½ Fat CARBOHYDRATE CHOICES: 1

not enough muffin pans?

If you don't have enough mini muffin pans to make the whole recipe, it's okay to cover and refrigerate some of the dough or batter while baking the first batch of desserts. Cool the pans about 15 minutes before baking the remaining desserts.

chocolate truffle brownie cups

prep time: **15 minutes**   *start to finish:* **1 hour 35 minutes**   [42 BROWNIE CUPS]

1 box (1 lb 2.3 oz) Betty Crocker fudge brownie mix

Water, vegetable oil and eggs called for on brownie mix box

⅔ cup whipping cream

6 oz semisweet baking chocolate, chopped

Chocolate candy sprinkles, if desired

1 Heat oven to 350°F. Place mini paper baking cup in each of 42 mini muffin cups.

2 In large bowl, stir brownie mix, water, oil and eggs until well blended. Fill muffin cups about ¾ full (about 1 tablespoon each) with batter.

3 Bake 19 to 21 minutes or until toothpick inserted into edge of brownie comes out clean. Cool 10 minutes before removing from pan. Cool completely, about 30 minutes.

4 In 1-quart saucepan, heat whipping cream over low heat just until hot but not boiling; remove from heat. Stir in baking chocolate until melted. Let stand about 15 minutes or until mixture coats spoon. (It will become firmer the longer it cools.) Spoon about 2 teaspoons chocolate mixture over each brownie. Sprinkle with candy sprinkles.

1 BROWNIE CUP: Calories 110; Total Fat 6g (Saturated Fat 2g; Trans Fat 0g); Cholesterol 15mg; Sodium 50mg; Total Carbohydrate 14g (Dietary Fiber 0g); Protein 0g EXCHANGES: 1 Other Carbohydrate, 1 Fat CARBOHYDRATE CHOICES: 1

sweet note Here's a nice variation on the original recipe. Add ½ teaspoon peppermint extract to the brownie batter. Then sprinkle crushed peppermint candies over the chocolate glaze at the end.

apricot petits fours

prep time: 1 hour 20 minutes   *start to finish:* 4 hours 20 minutes   [54 PETITS FOURS]

cake

1 box Betty Crocker
   SuperMoist yellow cake
   mix

1 cup apricot nectar or juice

⅓ cup vegetable oil

1 teaspoon grated orange
   peel

2 eggs

2 tablespoons orange-
   flavored liqueur or
   apricot nectar

icing

9 cups powdered sugar

¾ cup apricot nectar or
   water

½ cup corn syrup

⅓ cup butter or margarine,
   melted

2 teaspoons almond extract

decorations, if desired

Sliced almonds

Orange peel

1 Heat oven to 350°F (325°F for dark or nonstick pan). Spray bottom and sides of 15 × 10 × 1-inch pan with baking spray with flour.

2 In large bowl, beat all cake ingredients except liqueur with electric mixer on low speed 30 seconds. Beat on medium speed 2 minutes, scraping bowl occasionally. Pour batter into pan.

3 Bake 22 to 28 minutes or until cake springs back when lightly touched in center. Brush liqueur over top of cake. Cool completely, about 20 minutes. To avoid cake crumbs when adding icing, freeze cake 1 hour before cutting.

4 In large bowl, beat icing ingredients on low speed until powdered sugar is moistened. Beat on high speed until smooth. If necessary, add 2 to 3 teaspoons more apricot nectar until icing is pourable.

5 Place cooling rack on cookie sheet or waxed paper to catch icing drips. Cut cake into 9 rows by 6 rows. Working with 6 pieces at a time, remove cake pieces from pan and place on cooling rack. Spoon icing evenly over top and sides of cake pieces, letting icing coat sides. (Icing that drips off can be reused.) Let stand until icing is set, about 2 hours.

6 To make butterfly or flower decoration, arrange almonds on top of each frosted petit four (see photo). Cut small strips of orange peel and coat with coarse or granulated sugar; place piece in center of almonds as desired. Store in single layer in airtight plastic container at room temperature.

1 PETIT FOUR: Calories 160; Total Fat 3.5g (Saturated Fat 1.5g; Trans Fat 0g); Cholesterol 10mg; Sodium 75mg; Total Carbohydrate 31g (Dietary Fiber 0g); Protein 0g EXCHANGES: 2 Other Carbohydrate, 1 Fat CARBOHYDRATE CHOICES: 2

sweet note You can make these cakes up to 2 weeks ahead of time and freeze, but wait to add the icing until shortly before you serve them.

chocolate ganache mini cakes

prep time: **45 minutes** *start to finish:* **1 hour 55 minutes** [60 MINI CAKES]

mini cakes

1 box Betty Crocker SuperMoist devil's food cake mix

Water, vegetable oil and eggs called for on cake mix box

filling

⅔ cup raspberry jam

glaze and garnish

6 oz dark baking chocolate, chopped

⅔ cup whipping cream

1 tablespoon raspberry-flavored liqueur, if desired

Fresh raspberries, if desired

1   Heat oven to 350°F (325°F for dark or nonstick pans). Place mini paper baking cup in each of 60 mini muffin cups. Make cake mix as directed on box, using water, oil and eggs. Fill muffin cups ¾ full (about 1 heaping tablespoon each).

2   Bake 10 to 15 minutes or until toothpick inserted in center comes out clean. Cool in pans 5 minutes. Remove from pans to cooling racks. Cool completely, about 30 minutes.

3   By slowly spinning end of round handle of wooden spoon back and forth, make deep, ½-inch-wide indentation in center of top of each mini cake, not quite to bottom (wiggle end of spoon in mini cake to make opening large enough).

4   Spoon jam into small resealable food-storage plastic bag; seal bag. Cut ⅜-inch tip off 1 bottom corner of bag. Insert tip of bag into opening in each mini cake; squeeze bag to fill opening.

5   Place chocolate in medium bowl. In 1-quart saucepan, heat whipping cream just to boiling; pour over chocolate. Let stand 3 to 5 minutes until chocolate is melted and smooth when stirred. Stir in liqueur. Let stand 15 minutes, stirring occasionally, until mixture coats a spoon.

6   Spoon about 1 teaspoon chocolate glaze onto each mini cake. Garnish each with raspberry.

1 MINI CAKE: Calories 70; Total Fat 3g (Saturated Fat 1.5g; Trans Fat 0g); Cholesterol 0mg; Sodium 75mg; Total Carbohydrate 10g (Dietary Fiber 0g); Protein 0g EXCHANGES: ½ Other Carbohydrate, ½ Fat CARBOHYDRATE CHOICES: ½

sweet note If you refrigerate these little desserts, let them stand at room temperature at least 20 minutes before serving.

cherry mini cakes

prep time: **1 hour 50 minutes**   *start to finish:* **1 hour 50 minutes**   [60 MINI CAKES]

mini cakes

1 box Betty Crocker SuperMoist white cake mix

1 package (0.14 oz) cherry-flavored unsweetened soft drink mix

1¼ cups water

⅓ cup vegetable oil

1 teaspoon almond extract

3 egg whites

glaze

1 bag (2 lb) powdered sugar (8 cups)

½ cup water

½ cup corn syrup

2 teaspoons almond extract

2 to 3 teaspoons hot water

decoration

Miniature red candy hearts

1 Heat oven to 375°F (325°F for dark or nonstick pans). Grease bottoms only of 60 mini muffin cups with shortening or cooking spray.

2 In large bowl, beat all mini cake ingredients with electric mixer on low speed 30 seconds. Beat on medium speed 2 minutes, scraping bowl occasionally. Divide batter evenly among muffin cups (about ½ full). (If using one pan, refrigerate batter while baking other cakes; wash pan before filling with additional batter.)

3 Bake 10 to 13 minutes or until toothpick inserted in center comes out clean. Cool 5 minutes; remove cakes from muffin cups to cooling rack. Cool completely, about 30 minutes.

4 In 3-quart saucepan, mix all glaze ingredients except hot water. Heat over low heat, stirring frequently, until sugar is dissolved. Remove from heat. Stir in 2 teaspoons hot water. If necessary, stir in up to 1 teaspoon more water so glaze will just coat cakes.

5 Place cooling rack on cookie sheet or waxed paper to catch glaze drips. Turn each cake so top side is down on cooling rack. Pour about 1 tablespoon glaze over each cake, letting glaze coat sides. Let stand until glaze is set, about 15 minutes.

6 Top each cake with candy hearts. Store loosely covered at room temperature.

1 MINI CAKE: Calories 120; Total Fat 2g (Saturated Fat 0g; Trans Fat 0g); Cholesterol 0mg; Sodium 65mg; Total Carbohydrate 25g (Dietary Fiber 0g); Protein 0g EXCHANGES: 1½ Other Carbohydrate, ½ Fat CARBOHYDRATE CHOICES: 1½

sweet note Mini cakes like these are great for parties with a theme. You can pipe letters on the little cakes to say things such as "Congratulations" or "Bon Voyage."

citrus mini cheesecakes

prep time: **15 minutes**   *start to finish:* **1 hour 55 minutes**   [60 MINI CHEESECAKES]

crust

1½ cups Original Bisquick® mix

½ cup sugar

1 teaspoon grated lime, lemon or orange peel

⅓ cup cold butter or margarine

filling

3 packages (8 oz each) cream cheese, softened

1½ cups sugar

2 tablespoons Original Bisquick mix

1 teaspoon grated lime, lemon or orange peel

1¼ cups milk

3 tablespoons lime, lemon or orange juice

1 teaspoon vanilla

3 eggs

Citrus peel, if desired

1 Heat oven to 375°F.

2 In medium bowl, stir all crust ingredients except butter. With pastry blender or fork, cut in butter until mixture looks like coarse crumbs. Pat on bottom of ungreased 15 × 10 × 1-inch pan. Bake 10 minutes.

3 Meanwhile, in large bowl, beat cream cheese, 1½ cups sugar, 2 tablespoons Bisquick mix and 1 teaspoon lime peel with electric mixer on medium speed until blended and fluffy. On low speed, beat in milk, lime juice, vanilla and eggs until blended. Beat on low speed 2 minutes longer. Pour over partially baked crust.

4 Bake 35 to 40 minutes longer or until knife inserted in center comes out clean. Cool completely, about 1 hour. Refrigerate until ready to serve.

5 For mini cheesecakes, cut into 10 rows by 6 rows. Garnish with citrus peel. Store covered in refrigerator.

1 MINI CHEESECAKE: Calories 100; Total Fat 6g (Saturated Fat 3.5g; Trans Fat 0g); Cholesterol 25mg; Sodium 85mg; Total Carbohydrate 9g (Dietary Fiber 0g); Protein 2g EXCHANGES: ½ Other Carbohydrate, 1½ Fat CARBOHYDRATE CHOICES: ½

sweet note To cut these bars easily, use a knife dipped in a glass of water. Clean the knife and dip again in water when needed.

party perfect

Small desserts are the perfect ending for a variety of occasions and a great opportunity for extra-special garnishing. Arrange the desserts on your prettiest platter and surround with fresh seasonal fruit, edible flowers, a sprinkle of edible decorating glitter or pieces of citrus peel.

chapter two

cakes

fruit-topped almond cake

prep time: 15 minutes   *start to finish:* 1 hour 50 minutes   [8 SERVINGS]

cake

1¾ cups Betty Crocker SuperMoist yellow cake mix (from 1 lb 2.25-oz box)

½ cup water

½ cup slivered almonds, finely ground

3 tablespoons vegetable oil

½ teaspoon almond extract

2 eggs

topping

3 cups assorted fresh berries (such as raspberries, blueberries and blackberries)

¾ cup apricot preserves

3 tablespoons apple juice

3 tablespoons sliced almonds, toasted, if desired*

1 Heat oven to 350°F (325°F for dark or nonstick pan). Generously spray bottom and side of 8- or 9-inch round cake pan with baking spray with flour.

2 In large bowl, beat all cake ingredients with electric mixer on low speed until moistened. Beat on medium speed 2 minutes, scraping bowl occasionally. Pour into pan.

3 Bake 24 to 29 minutes or until toothpick inserted in center comes out clean. Cool 10 minutes; remove cake from pan to cooling rack. Cool completely, about 1 hour.

4 Place berries in medium bowl. In 1-quart saucepan, heat preserves and apple juice to boiling, stirring frequently. Pour over berries; toss until coated. Let stand 5 minutes.

5 Level top of cake, using serrated knife. Place cake on serving plate, sliced side down. Arrange berries on cake; drizzle with syrup remaining in bowl. Sprinkle with sliced almonds. Store covered in refrigerator.

*To toast almonds, bake in ungreased shallow pan in 350°F oven about 10 minutes, stirring occasionally, until golden brown.

1 SERVING: Calories 320; Total Fat 12g (Saturated Fat 2g; Trans Fat 0.5g); Cholesterol 55mg; Sodium 200mg; Total Carbohydrate 49g (Dietary Fiber 4g); Protein 4g EXCHANGES: 1½ Starch, 1½ Other Carbohydrate, 2½ Fat CARBOHYDRATE CHOICES: 3

sweet note Grind the slivered almonds for the cake in a small food processor, or chop them very finely with a knife.

ooey-gooey caramel cake

prep time: 20 minutes *start to finish:* 2 hours 5 minutes [15 SERVINGS]

1 box (1 lb 2.25 oz) Betty
  Crocker SuperMoist
  yellow cake mix

¼ cup all-purpose flour

1 cup water

⅓ cup vegetable oil

3 eggs

1 bag (8 oz) milk chocolate-
  coated toffee bits

1 can (13.4 oz) dulce de
  leche (caramelized
  sweetened condensed
  milk)

Sweetened whipped cream,
  if desired

Caramel topping, if desired

1 Heat oven to 350°F (325°F for dark or nonstick pan). Spray bottom and sides of 13 × 9-inch pan with baking spray with flour.

2 In large bowl, beat cake mix, flour, water, oil and eggs with electric mixer on low speed 30 seconds. Beat on medium speed 2 minutes, scraping bowl occasionally. Stir in ½ cup of the toffee bits. Pour into pan.

3 Reserve ½ cup dulce de leche. Spoon remaining dulce de leche by teaspoonfuls onto batter.

4 Bake 30 to 40 minutes or until toothpick inserted in center comes out clean. Cool 5 minutes. Drop reserved dulce de leche by spoonfuls over top of cake and spread evenly. Sprinkle with remaining toffee bits. Cool about 1 hour before serving. Top each serving with whipped cream and caramel topping.

1 SERVING: Calories 370; Total Fat 14g (Saturated Fat 6g; Trans Fat 1g); Cholesterol 55mg; Sodium 310mg; Total Carbohydrate 54g (Dietary Fiber 0g); Protein 5g EXCHANGES: 1½ Starch, 2 Other Carbohydrate, 2½ Fat CARBOHYDRATE CHOICES: 3½

sweet note Crushed, chocolate-covered English toffee candy bars can be used instead of the toffee bits.

premium tres leches cake

prep time: **15 minutes**   *start to finish:* **1 hour 55 minutes**   [15 SERVINGS]

1 box (1 lb 2.25 oz) Betty
Crocker SuperMoist
yellow cake mix

1¼ cups water

1 tablespoon vegetable oil

2 teaspoons vanilla

4 eggs

1 can (14 oz) sweetened
condensed milk (not
evaporated)

1 cup whole milk or
evaporated milk

1 cup whipping cream

1 container (12 oz) fluffy
white whipped ready-to-
spread frosting

Cut-up fresh fruit, if desired

1 Heat oven to 350°F (325°F for dark or nonstick pan). Grease bottom and sides of 13 × 9-inch pan with shortening or cooking spray.

2 In large bowl, beat cake mix, water, oil, vanilla and eggs with electric mixer on low speed 30 seconds. Beat on medium speed 2 minutes, scraping bowl occasionally. Pour into pan.

3 Bake 29 to 35 minutes or until edges are golden brown and tooth-pick inserted in center comes out clean. Let stand 5 minutes. With long-tined fork, poke top of hot cake every ½ inch, wiping fork occasionally to reduce sticking.

4 In large bowl, stir together condensed milk, whole milk and whipping cream. Carefully pour evenly over top of cake. Cover; refrigerate about 1 hour or until mixture is absorbed into cake. Spread with frosting. Top with fresh fruit.

1 SERVING: Calories 410; Total Fat 18g (Saturated Fat 8g; Trans Fat 2.5g); Cholesterol 85mg; Sodium 310mg; Total Carbohydrate 58g (Dietary Fiber 0g); Protein 5g EXCHANGES: 1 Starch, 3 Other Carbohydrate, 3½ Fat CARBOHYDRATE CHOICES: 4

sweet note *Tres leches* is the Spanish term for three milks. The three types of milk create this cake's signature indulgence and moistness.

raspberry crumb cake

prep time: 20 minutes   *start to finish:* 1 hour 30 minutes   [9 SERVINGS]

cake

1¾ cups Betty Crocker SuperMoist yellow cake mix (from 1 lb 2.25-oz box)

⅓ cup sour cream

2 tablespoons all-purpose flour

2 tablespoons vegetable oil

2 tablespoons water

1 egg

¾ cup fresh raspberries

topping

½ cup sugar

⅓ cup sliced almonds

3 tablespoons all-purpose flour

3 tablespoons butter or margarine, softened

garnish, if desired

Fresh raspberries

Fresh mint leaves

1 Heat oven to 350°F (325°F for dark or nonstick pan). Spray bottom and sides of 8- or 9-inch square pan with baking spray with flour.

2 In large bowl, beat all cake ingredients except raspberries with electric mixer on low speed 30 seconds. Beat on medium speed 2 minutes, scraping bowl occasionally. Spread in pan. Place raspberries on top of batter.

3 In small bowl, stir topping ingredients until well mixed. Sprinkle evenly over batter and raspberries.

4 Bake 28 to 38 minutes or until toothpick inserted in center comes out clean. Cool at least 30 minutes before serving. Garnish with fresh raspberries and mint leaves.

1 SERVING: Calories 270; Total Fat 13g (Saturated Fat 5g; Trans Fat 1g); Cholesterol 40mg; Sodium 190mg; Total Carbohydrate 35g (Dietary Fiber 1g); Protein 3g EXCHANGES: 1 Starch, 1½ Other Carbohydrate, 2 Fat CARBOHYDRATE CHOICES: 2

sweet note Frozen berries without syrup or sugar, thawed and drained, can be used in place of the fresh raspberries.

caramel latte cake

prep time: 30 minutes   *start to finish:* 3 hours 20 minutes   [16 SERVINGS]

cake

1 box (1 lb 2.25 oz) Betty Crocker SuperMoist yellow cake mix

1¼ cups warm water

1 tablespoon instant espresso coffee granules

⅓ cup butter or margarine, melted

3 eggs

filling

1 can (13.4 oz) dulce de leche (caramelized sweetened condensed milk)

½ cup hot water

3 tablespoons instant espresso coffee granules

1 tablespoon dark rum or 1 teaspoon rum extract plus 2 teaspoons water

frosting and garnish

1 cup whipping cream

¼ cup powdered sugar

1 teaspoon unsweetened baking cocoa or 2 oz semisweet baking chocolate, chopped

1 Heat oven to 350°F (325°F for dark or nonstick pan). Spray bottom only of 13 × 9-inch pan with baking spray with flour.

2 In large bowl, place cake mix. In 2-cup glass measuring cup, stir 1¼ cups warm water and 1 tablespoon espresso granules until granules are dissolved. Add espresso mixture, butter and eggs to cake mix. Beat with electric mixer on low speed 30 seconds. Beat on medium speed 2 minutes, scraping bowl occasionally. Pour into pan.

3 Bake 30 to 35 minutes or until toothpick inserted in center comes out clean. Cool cake in pan on cooling rack 15 minutes.

4 Meanwhile, pour dulce de leche into medium microwavable bowl. In small bowl, mix ½ cup hot water, 3 tablespoons espresso granules and the rum; stir into dulce de leche until smooth. Microwave uncovered on High 2 to 3 minutes, stirring after about 1 minute with whisk, until pourable. Set aside while cake cools.

5 With wooden spoon handle (¼ to ½ inch in diameter), poke cooled cake every ½ inch, wiping handle occasionally to reduce sticking. Pour dulce de leche mixture evenly over cake; spread mixture over top of cake with metal spatula to fill holes. Run knife around sides of pan to loosen cake. Cover; refrigerate 2 hours.

6 In medium bowl, beat whipping cream and powdered sugar on high speed until stiff peaks form. Spread whipped cream evenly over chilled cake. Sprinkle evenly with cocoa. Store covered in refrigerator.

1 SERVING: Calories 330; Total Fat 14g (Saturated Fat 8g; Trans Fat 1g); Cholesterol 65mg; Sodium 280mg; Total Carbohydrate 45g (Dietary Fiber 0g); Protein 4g EXCHANGES: 1 Starch, 2 Other Carbohydrate, 3 Fat CARBOHYDRATE CHOICES: 3

sweet note Place the cocoa in a tea strainer and lightly shake over the frosting to "dust" the top of the cake.

chocolate-caramel-nut cake

prep time: **15 minutes**   *start to finish:* **2 hours 35 minutes**   [16 SERVINGS]

1 box (1 lb 2.25 oz) Betty Crocker SuperMoist butter recipe chocolate cake mix

1 box (4-serving size) chocolate instant pudding and pie filling mix

1 cup water

½ cup butter or margarine, softened

4 eggs

1 cup semisweet chocolate chips

⅓ cup caramel topping

2 tablespoons chopped nuts

1 Heat oven to 350°F (325°F for fluted tube cake, dark or nonstick pan). Grease and flour 12-cup fluted tube cake pan or 10 × 4-inch angel food (tube cake) pan, or spray with baking spray with flour.

2 In large bowl, beat cake mix, pudding mix, water, butter and eggs with electric mixer on low speed 30 seconds, then on medium speed 2 minutes, scraping bowl occasionally. Stir in chocolate chips. Pour into pan.

3 Bake 50 to 55 minutes or until toothpick inserted in center comes out clean. Cool 15 minutes in pan. Remove from pan to plate. Cool 10 minutes. Prick top of warm cake several times with fork; spread caramel topping over top of cake. Sprinkle with nuts. Cool completely, about 1 hour. Store covered.

1 SERVING: Calories 310; Total Fat 13g (Saturated Fat 7g; Trans Fat 0.5g); Cholesterol 70mg; Sodium 430mg; Total Carbohydrate 43g (Dietary Fiber 2g); Protein 4g EXCHANGES: 1 Starch, 2 Other Carbohydrate, 2½ Fat CARBOHYDRATE CHOICES: 3

sweet note Can't get enough of the good stuff? Pass bowls of caramel topping and extra chopped nuts for an extra-rich hit.

chocolate mousse–raspberry cake

prep time: **25 minutes**   *start to finish:* **3 hours 15 minutes**   [16 SERVINGS]

1 box (1 lb 2.25 oz) Betty Crocker SuperMoist devil's food cake mix

Water, vegetable oil and eggs called for on cake mix box

1 cup semisweet chocolate chips (6 oz)

1½ cups whipping cream

⅓ cup powdered sugar

2 tablespoons seedless raspberry jam

1 container (6 oz) fresh raspberries

White chocolate truffle candies, if desired

Cocoa, if desired

1 Heat oven to 350°F (325°F for dark or nonstick pans). Spray bottoms and sides of 2 (8- or 9-inch) round cake pans with baking spray with flour.

2 Make cake mix as directed on box, using water, oil and eggs. Pour into pans.

3 Bake 24 to 29 minutes or until toothpick inserted in center comes out clean. Cool 10 minutes; remove cakes from pans to cooling rack. Cool completely, about 1 hour.

4 Meanwhile, in medium microwavable bowl, microwave chocolate chips and ½ cup of the whipping cream uncovered on High 45 to 60 seconds; stir until smooth and melted. Refrigerate 15 to 30 minutes or until cool.

5 In large bowl, beat remaining 1 cup whipping cream and the powdered sugar with electric mixer on high speed until mixture starts to thicken. Add melted chocolate. Beat until stiff peaks form (do not overbeat or mixture will begin to look curdled).

6 On serving plate, place 1 cake layer, rounded side down. Spread raspberry jam over cake layer. Spread ½-inch-thick layer of chocolate mixture over jam. Cut ½ cup of the raspberries in half; press into chocolate mixture. Add second cake layer, rounded side up; press lightly. Frost side and top of cake with remaining chocolate mixture. Refrigerate about 1 hour or until firm.

7 To serve, let stand at room temperature about 10 minutes. Garnish with remaining raspberries and candies; sprinkle with cocoa. Store in refrigerator.

sweet note You could simply garnish the cake with the remaining raspberries and fresh mint leaves if you prefer.

1 SERVING: Calories 350; Total Fat 20g (Saturated Fat 9g; Trans Fat 0.5g); Cholesterol 65mg; Sodium 280mg; Total Carbohydrate 39g (Dietary Fiber 2g); Protein 4g EXCHANGES: 1 Starch, 1½ Other Carbohydrate, 4 Fat CARBOHYDRATE CHOICES: 2½

chocolate chai latte cake

prep time: **15 minutes**   *start to finish:* **1 hour 55 minutes**   [15 SERVINGS]

cake

1 box (1 lb 2.25 oz) Betty Crocker SuperMoist devil's food cake mix

¼ cup chai latte–flavored international instant coffee mix (from 9.7-oz container)

1⅓ cups water

½ cup vegetable oil

3 eggs

1 cup miniature semisweet chocolate chips

frosting

2½ cups powdered sugar

2 tablespoons butter or margarine, softened

3 tablespoons milk

1 tablespoon chai latte–flavored international instant coffee mix (from 9.7-oz container)

Ground cinnamon, if desired

1 Heat oven to 350°F (325°F for dark or nonstick pan). Spray bottom and sides of 13 × 9-inch pan with baking spray with flour.

2 In large bowl, beat cake mix, ¼ cup dry chai latte mix, the water, oil and eggs with electric mixer on low speed 30 seconds. Beat on medium speed 2 minutes, scraping bowl occasionally. Stir in chocolate chips. Pour into pan.

3 Bake 29 to 39 minutes or until center of cake springs back when lightly touched. Cool completely, about 1 hour. (A crack may appear in top of cake, but frosting will cover it.)

4 In medium bowl, mix powdered sugar and butter until smooth; set aside. In small microwavable bowl, microwave milk on High 10 to 15 seconds until very warm. Stir in 1 tablespoon dry chai latte mix until dissolved; stir into powdered sugar mixture until smooth and spreadable. Frost cake. Just before serving, sprinkle with cinnamon.

1 SERVING: Calories 390; Total Fat 16g (Saturated Fat 5g; Trans Fat 1g); Cholesterol 45mg; Sodium 340mg; Total Carbohydrate 56g (Dietary Fiber 1g); Protein 3g EXCHANGES: 1 Starch, 2½ Other Carbohydrate, 3½ Fat CARBOHYDRATE CHOICES: 4

cutting frosted cakes

Follow these tips for perfect cake servings every time.

- **Use a sharp, thin knife** to cut most cakes.

- **Use a long serrated knife** for angel food cakes.

- **If frosting sticks,** dip the knife in hot water; wipe with a damp paper towel after cutting each piece.

sweet note Look for the chai latte mix near the coffee at the grocery store.

deep dark mocha torte

prep time: 50 minutes   *start to finish:* 3 hours   [16 SERVINGS]

torte

1 box (1 lb 2.25 oz) Betty Crocker SuperMoist chocolate fudge cake mix

Water, vegetable oil and eggs called for on cake mix box

⅓ cup granulated sugar

⅓ cup rum or water

1¼ teaspoons instant espresso coffee granules

filling

2 packages (8 oz each) cream cheese, softened

1 cup powdered sugar

1 teaspoon vanilla

2 to 3 teaspoons milk

ganache

1½ cups semisweet chocolate chips

6 tablespoons butter (do not use margarine)

⅓ cup whipping cream

sweet note If the ganache becomes too thick to spread, let it stand at room temperature for a few minutes, then stir to soften.

1 Heat oven to 350°F (325°F for dark or nonstick pans). Spray bottoms only of 2 (8- or 9-inch) round cake pans with baking spray with flour.

2 Make cake mix as directed on box, using water, oil and eggs. Pour batter into pans.

3 Bake as directed on box for 8- or 9-inch round pans. Cool 10 minutes; remove from pans to cooling rack. Cool completely, about 1 hour.

4 Meanwhile, in 1-quart saucepan, stir granulated sugar, rum and coffee granules until coffee is dissolved. Heat to boiling, stirring occasionally; remove from heat. Cool completely.

5 In medium bowl, beat filling ingredients with electric mixer on low speed just until blended, adding enough milk for spreading consistency; set aside.

6 In 1-quart saucepan, heat ganache ingredients over low heat, stirring frequently, until chips are melted and mixture is smooth. Refrigerate about 30 minutes, stirring occasionally, until slightly thickened.

7 To assemble cake, cut each layer in half horizontally. Brush about 1 tablespoon of the rum mixture over cut side of each layer half; let stand 1 minute to soak into cake. Place 1 layer half on serving plate; spread with about ⅔ cup filling. Repeat with remaining 3 layers and filling. Spread ganache over side and top of torte. Store loosely covered in refrigerator.

1 SERVING: Calories 660; Total Fat 41g (Saturated Fat 20g; Trans Fat 1.5g); Cholesterol 115mg; Sodium 520mg; Total Carbohydrate 64g (Dietary Fiber 2g); Protein 7g EXCHANGES: 1 Starch, 3½ Other Carbohydrate, ½ High-Fat Meat, 7 Fat CARBOHYDRATE CHOICES: 4

fudge lover's strawberry truffle cake

prep time: 25 minutes   *start to finish:* 2 hours 50 minutes   [12 SERVINGS]

cake

1 box (1 lb 2.25 oz) Betty Crocker SuperMoist chocolate fudge cake mix

Water, vegetable oil and eggs called for on cake mix box

ganache filling and topping

2 packages (8 oz each) semisweet baking chocolate, finely chopped

1⅓ cups whipping cream

¼ cup butter (do not use margarine)

2 cups cut-up fresh strawberries

garnish

6 fresh strawberries, cut in half lengthwise through stem

¼ cup white vanilla baking chips

½ teaspoon vegetable oil

sweet note Impress your friends with this decadent chocolate and strawberry dessert. Save the six prettiest strawberries for the garnish.

1 Heat oven to 350°F (325°F for dark or nonstick pan). Grease bottom only of 13 × 9-inch pan with shortening or cooking spray.

2 Make cake mix as directed on box, using water, oil and eggs. Bake as directed on box for 13 × 9-inch pan. Cool completely, about 1 hour.

3 Meanwhile, in large bowl, place chopped chocolate; set aside. In 2-quart saucepan, heat whipping cream and butter over medium heat, stirring occasionally, until butter is melted and mixture comes to a boil. Pour cream mixture over chocolate; stir until smooth.

4 Line bottom of 9-inch springform pan with waxed paper round. Cut cake into 1-inch cubes. In large bowl, beat half of the cake cubes on low speed until cake is crumbly. Add remaining cake cubes and 1¾ cups of the ganache (reserve remaining ganache for topping). Beat on low speed 30 seconds, then on medium speed until well combined (mixture will look like fudge). Fold in 2 cups cut-up strawberries. Spoon mixture into springform pan; smooth top. Cover with plastic wrap; freeze 45 minutes or until firm enough to unmold.

5 Run knife around side of pan to loosen cake mixture. Place serving plate upside down on pan; turn pan and plate over. Frost side and top of cake with reserved ganache. Arrange strawberry halves on top of cake.

6 In small microwavable bowl, microwave baking chips and ½ teaspoon oil uncovered on High 45 seconds, stirring every 15 seconds, until melted. Place in small resealable food-storage plastic bag; cut off tiny corner of bag. Drizzle over top of cake. Refrigerate until ready to serve. Cake is best served the same day.

1 SERVING: Calories 630; Total Fat 38g (Saturated Fat 18g; Trans Fat 1g); Cholesterol 95mg; Sodium 410mg; Total Carbohydrate 65g (Dietary Fiber 4g); Protein 6g EXCHANGES: ½ Starch, 4 Other Carbohydrate, ½ High-Fat Meat, 6½ Fat CARBOHYDRATE CHOICES: 4

chocolate-orange truffle cake

prep time: **15 minutes**   *start to finish:* **3 hours**   [16 SERVINGS]

1 box (1 lb 2.25 oz) Betty Crocker SuperMoist chocolate fudge cake mix

Water, vegetable oil and eggs called for on cake mix box

1 tablespoon grated orange peel

1 container (1 lb) chocolate creamy ready-to-spread frosting

⅓ cup whipping cream

½ cup semisweet chocolate chips

1   Heat oven to 350°F (325°F for dark or nonstick pans). Spray bottoms only of 2 (8- or 9-inch) round cake pans with baking spray with flour.

2   Make cake mix as directed on box, using water, oil and eggs; add orange peel to batter. Pour into pans.

3   Bake as directed on box for 8- or 9-inch round pans. Cool 10 minutes; remove cakes from pans to cooling rack. Cool completely, about 1 hour.

4   Level cake tops if necessary with serrated knife. Place one cake layer on serving plate; spread with frosting. Top with second layer; frost top and side of cake.

5   In 1-quart saucepan, heat whipping cream over medium heat until hot (do not boil); remove from heat. Stir in chocolate chips until melted and smooth. Let stand 5 minutes. Carefully pour chocolate mixture on top center of cake; spread to edge, allowing some to drizzle down side. Refrigerate about 1 hour or until chocolate is set. Store covered in refrigerator.

1 SERVING: Calories 370; Total Fat 19g (Saturated Fat 6g; Trans Fat 2.5g); Cholesterol 45mg; Sodium 350mg; Total Carbohydrate 45g (Dietary Fiber 1g); Protein 3g   EXCHANGES: 1 Starch, 2 Other Carbohydrate, 3½ Fat   CARBOHYDRATE CHOICES: 3

frosting secrets

These simple success tips make frosting layer cakes easier.

- **Freeze the cake** for 30 to 60 minutes before frosting.
- **Place a dab of frosting** under the cake on the serving plate to keep the cake from sliding.
- **Place strips of waxed paper** under the cake edge.
- **Use a thin metal spatula** to spread the frosting easily.
- **Use a light touch** to prevent layers from sliding and the filling from squishing out between layers.

sweet note To keep the edge of the plate clean while frosting the cake, place several strips of waxed paper around the edge of the plate, place the cake on the paper, frost the cake, then carefully remove and discard the strips.

mud slide ice cream cake

prep time: **30 minutes**   *start to finish:* **6 hours**   [15 SERVINGS]

1 box (1 lb 2.25 oz) Betty Crocker SuperMoist chocolate fudge cake mix

½ cup butter or margarine, melted

2 eggs

2 tablespoons coffee-flavored liqueur or prepared strong coffee

4 cups vanilla ice cream

1 container (12 oz) chocolate whipped ready-to-spread frosting

2 tablespoons coffee-flavored liqueur, if desired

1 Heat oven to 350°F (325°F for dark or nonstick pan). Spray bottom only of 13 × 9-inch pan with baking spray with flour.

2 In large bowl, beat cake mix, butter and eggs with electric mixer on medium speed until well blended. Spread batter in pan.

3 Bake 19 to 24 minutes or until center is set (top will appear dry and cracked). Cool completely, about 1 hour.

4 Brush 2 tablespoons liqueur over cake. Let ice cream stand at room temperature about 15 minutes to soften. Spread ice cream over cake. Freeze 3 hours or until firm.

5 In medium bowl, mix frosting and 2 tablespoons liqueur; spread over ice cream. Freeze at least 1 hour. Store covered in freezer.

1 SERVING: Calories 390; Total Fat 18g (Saturated Fat 9g; Trans Fat 1.5g); Cholesterol 60mg; Sodium 410mg; Total Carbohydrate 51g (Dietary Fiber 2g); Protein 4g EXCHANGES: 1 Starch, 2½ Other Carbohydrate, 3½ Fat CARBOHYDRATE CHOICES: 3½

sweet note This yummy dessert has a fudgy brownie base. Coffee lovers can substitute coffee-flavored ice cream for the vanilla.

berry cream torte

prep time: **25** minutes *start to finish:* **2** hours **10** minutes [16 SERVINGS]

1 box (1 lb 2.25 oz) Betty Crocker SuperMoist white cake mix

Water, vegetable oil and egg whites called for on cake mix box

2 containers (12 oz each) fluffy white whipped ready-to-spread frosting

1 container (8 oz) frozen whipped topping, thawed

1 cup fresh raspberries

1 cup fresh blueberries

1 cup sliced fresh strawberries

¼ cup seedless strawberry jam

1 tablespoon orange juice

1 Heat oven to 350°F (325°F for dark or nonstick pans).

2 Make and bake cake mix as directed on box for two 8- or 9-inch round cake pans, using water, oil and eggs. Cool 10 minutes; remove from pans to cooling rack. Cool completely, about 1 hour.

3 In large bowl, mix frosting and whipped topping until well blended. To assemble cake, cut each layer in half horizontally. Place 1 layer half on serving plate; spread with 1 cup of the frosting mixture. Repeat 3 more times. Arrange berries on top of cake.

4 In small microwavable bowl, microwave jam uncovered on High about 20 seconds or until warm. Stir in orange juice; mix well with fork. Brush over berries. Store in refrigerator.

1 SERVING: Calories 430; Total Fat 19g (Saturated Fat 6g; Trans Fat 3.5g); Cholesterol 0mg; Sodium 280mg; Total Carbohydrate 61g (Dietary Fiber 1g); Protein 3g EXCHANGES: 1 Starch, 3 Other Carbohydrate, 3½ Fat CARBOHYDRATE CHOICES: 4

sweet note If you don't have a cake dome to store the cake, use plastic wrap; but first insert toothpicks all over the cake to keep the wrap from sticking to the frosting.

banana turtle torte

prep time: **30 minutes**   *start to finish:* **5 hours 15 minutes**   [16 SERVINGS]

1 box (1 lb 2.25 oz) Betty Crocker SuperMoist German chocolate cake mix

Water, vegetable oil and eggs called for on cake mix box

1½ cups whipping cream

3 bananas

1 cup butterscotch caramel topping

6 tablespoons chopped pecans, toasted*

sweet note For a pretty serving presentation, drizzle caramel topping in a pretty pattern on each plate. Center a slice of torte on the plate, then place a dollop of whipped cream topped with a pecan half next to it.

1 Heat oven to 350°F (325°F for dark or nonstick pans). Grease bottoms only of 2 (9-inch) round cake pans with shortening or cooking spray.

2 Make cake mix as directed on box, using water, oil and eggs. Pour into pans.

3 Bake as directed on box for 9-inch round pans. Cool 10 minutes; remove cakes from pans to cooling rack. Cool completely, about 1 hour. If desired, freeze cakes uncovered about 1 hour for easier cutting and frosting.

4 In chilled medium bowl, beat whipping cream on high speed until stiff peaks form.

5 Cut each cake horizontally to make 2 layers. (Mark side of cake with toothpicks and cut with long, thin knife.) On serving plate, place top layer of first cake, cut side up. Spread ⅔ cup whipped cream over layer to within ¼ inch of edge. Slice 1 banana; arrange on whipped cream, overlapping slices if necessary. Drizzle ¼ cup butterscotch caramel topping over banana, spreading to coat slices. Sprinkle with 2 tablespoons pecans.

6 Top with bottom layer of first cake, cut side down. Spread with ⅔ cup whipped cream, 1 sliced banana, ¼ cup butterscotch caramel topping and 2 tablespoons pecans. Top with bottom layer of second cake, cut side up. Repeat filling. Top with top layer of second cake, cut side down.

7 Frost top of torte with remaining whipped cream. Spoon remaining butterscotch caramel topping over whipped cream. Swirl caramel into whipped cream with tip of knife. Cover; refrigerate about 2 hours or until ready to serve. For best results, serve torte the same day.

To toast pecans, bake in an ungreased shallow pan in a 350°F oven about 10 minutes, stirring occasionally, until golden brown.

1 SERVING: Calories 370; Total Fat 19g (Saturated Fat 7g; Trans Fat 0.5g); Cholesterol 65mg; Sodium 340mg; Total Carbohydrate 46g (Dietary Fiber 2g); Protein 4g EXCHANGES: 1 Starch, 2 Other Carbohydrate, 3½ Fat CARBOHYDRATE CHOICES: 3

strawberries 'n cream cake

prep time: **15** minutes   *start to finish:* **1 hour 40 minutes**   [15 SERVINGS]

1 box (1 lb 2.25 oz) Betty Crocker SuperMoist white cake mix

1¼ cups half-and-half

1 tablespoon vegetable oil

4 eggs

½ cup strawberry syrup

1 container (8 oz) frozen whipped topping, thawed

3 cups fresh whole strawberries, sliced

¼ cup strawberry jam

2 tablespoons sugar

1 Heat oven to 350°F (325°F for dark or nonstick pan). Spray bottom and sides of 13 × 9-inch pan with baking spray with flour.

2 In large bowl, beat cake mix, half-and-half, oil and eggs with electric mixer on low speed 30 seconds. Beat on medium speed 2 minutes, scraping bowl occasionally. Pour into pan.

3 Bake 25 to 30 minutes or until toothpick inserted in center comes out clean. Cool 20 minutes. With tines of meat fork or a table knife, poke cake every inch. Pour strawberry syrup slowly over cake, allowing syrup to fill holes in cake. Cool completely, about 35 minutes longer.

4 Spread whipped topping over cake. In medium bowl, gently mix strawberries, jam and sugar. Top each serving with strawberry mixture. Store covered cake and strawberry mixture separately in refrigerator.

1 SERVING: Calories 270; Total Fat 11g (Saturated Fat 6g; Trans Fat 1g); Cholesterol 65mg; Sodium 260mg; Total Carbohydrate 40g (Dietary Fiber 1g); Protein 4g EXCHANGES: 1 Fruit, 1½ Other Carbohydrate, ½ Medium-Fat Meat, 1½ Fat CARBOHYDRATE CHOICES: 2½

sweet note Using a meat fork to poke the cake works well because the tines are longer and larger, ensuring better saturation of the syrup in the cake. Be sure to take your time pouring the syrup over the cake, letting it seep down into the holes.

easy grease and flour

The next time a recipe directs you to grease and flour a baking pan, try baking spray with flour, available in aerosol cans in the baking aisle of the grocery store. This one-step item is easier and less messy than the alternative.

coconut cake with white chocolate frosting

prep time: **25 minutes**   *start to finish:* **2 hours**   [15 SERVINGS]

1 can (14 oz) coconut milk
(not cream of coconut)

1 box (1 lb 2.25 oz) Betty
Crocker SuperMoist
white cake mix

¼ cup water

3 egg whites

¾ cup flaked coconut

1 cup white vanilla baking
chips (6 oz)

1¾ cups powdered sugar

⅓ cup butter or margarine,
softened

½ teaspoon vanilla

sweet note The
larger flaked coconut is great
for this cake, but you can use
regular flaked or shredded
coconut instead.

1   Heat oven to 350°F (325°F for dark or nonstick pan). Spray bottom
only of 13 × 9-inch pan with baking spray with flour.

2   Reserve ⅓ cup coconut milk for frosting. In large bowl, beat cake
mix, remaining coconut milk (1⅓ cups), the water and egg whites
with electric mixer on low speed 30 seconds. Beat on medium speed
2 minutes, scraping bowl occasionally. Stir in ½ cup of the coconut
until well combined. Pour into pan.

3   Bake 28 to 33 minutes or until toothpick inserted in center comes
out clean. Cool completely, about 1 hour.

4   Meanwhile, in 2-quart microwavable bowl, microwave vanilla baking
chips uncovered on High 30 seconds or until melted. Stir; if chips
are not completely melted, microwave 15 seconds longer, then stir
until all chips are melted. Stir in powdered sugar, butter, reserved
⅓ cup coconut milk and the vanilla. Cover; refrigerate 30 to 60 minutes.
(If frosting becomes too firm to spread, microwave uncovered on
High 10 to 15 seconds to soften; stir until smooth.)

5   Spread frosting over cake. Immediately sprinkle top with remaining
¼ cup coconut. Store loosely covered at room temperature.

1 SERVING: Calories 370; Total Fat 16g (Saturated Fat 11g; Trans Fat 1g); Cholesterol 10mg;
Sodium 320mg; Total Carbohydrate 51g (Dietary Fiber 0g); Protein 4g EXCHANGES: 1 Starch,
2½ Other Carbohydrate, 3 Fat CARBOHYDRATE CHOICES: 3½

key lime pie poke cake

prep time: 20 minutes   *start to finish:* 1 hour 55 minutes   [15 SERVINGS]

cake

1 box (1 lb 2.25 oz) Betty Crocker SuperMoist white cake mix

1¼ cups water

1 tablespoon vegetable oil

4 eggs

filling

1 can (14 oz) sweetened condensed milk (not evaporated)

¾ cup whipping cream

½ cup Key lime juice or regular lime juice

1 teaspoon grated lime peel

4 drops yellow food color

1 drop green food color

frosting

1 container (12 oz) vanilla whipped ready-to-spread frosting

2 teaspoons grated lime peel

garnish, if desired

Fresh strawberries

Key lime slices

Lemon leaves

1 Heat oven to 350°F (325°F for dark or nonstick pan). Spray bottom only of 13 × 9-inch pan with baking spray with flour.

2 In large bowl, beat cake ingredients with electric mixer on low speed 30 seconds. Beat on medium speed 2 minutes, scraping bowl occasionally. Pour into pan.

3 Bake 26 to 30 minutes or until toothpick inserted in center comes out clean. Cool 5 minutes. With handle of wooden spoon (¼ to ½ inch in diameter), poke holes almost to bottom of cake every ½ inch, wiping spoon handle occasionally to reduce sticking.

4 In medium bowl, stir together filling ingredients (mixture will thicken). Pour over cake; spread evenly over surface, working back and forth to fill holes. (Some filling should remain on top of cake.) Refrigerate 1 hour.

5 Spread frosting over cake; sprinkle with lime peel. Garnish with strawberries, lime slices and lemon leaves. Store loosely covered in refrigerator.

1 SERVING: Calories 390; Total Fat 16g (Saturated Fat 7g; Trans Fat 2.5g); Cholesterol 80mg; Sodium 310mg; Total Carbohydrate 56g (Dietary Fiber 0g); Protein 6g EXCHANGES: ½ Starch, 3 Other Carbohydrate, ½ High-Fat Meat, 2½ Fat CARBOHYDRATE CHOICES: 4

sweet note Key lime juice is not green, so if you'd prefer a greener filling in this cake, add a couple drops of green food color to the filling before pouring it over the cake. You'll find Key lime juice near the other bottled lime juices in the grocery store.

mango-strawberry sorbet torte

prep time: 35 minutes   *start to finish:* 5 hours   [16 SERVINGS]

cake

1 box (1 lb 2.25 oz) Betty Crocker SuperMoist white cake mix

Water, vegetable oil and egg whites called for on cake mix box

1 pint (2 cups) mango sorbet, softened

1 pint (2 cups) strawberry sorbet, softened

frosting

1½ cups whipping cream

½ cup powdered sugar

1 teaspoon grated lime peel

2 tablespoons lime juice

garnish, if desired

Lime peel twists

White chocolate–dipped fresh strawberries

1 Heat oven to 350°F (325°F for dark or nonstick pan). Spray bottom only of 15 × 10 × 1-inch pan with baking spray with flour. Line with waxed paper; spray waxed paper.

2 Make cake mix as directed on box, using water, oil and egg whites. Pour into pan.

3 Bake 20 to 30 minutes or until toothpick inserted in center comes out clean. Cool 10 minutes; remove cake from pan to cooling rack and remove waxed paper. Cool completely, about 1 hour.

4 Cut cake crosswise into 3 equal sections. On long serving platter, place 1 section, rounded side down. Spread mango sorbet evenly over top. Place another cake section on sorbet; press down. Spread with strawberry sorbet. Top with remaining cake section; press down. Cover lightly; freeze about 2 hours or until firm.

5 In large bowl, beat frosting ingredients with electric mixer on high speed until stiff peaks form. Frost sides and top of torte. Freeze about 1 hour or until firm.

6 To serve, let stand at room temperature 10 minutes. Garnish top with lime peel and strawberries. Cut torte in half lengthwise, then cut crosswise 8 times to make a total of 16 slices.

1 SERVING: Calories 330; Total Fat 15g (Saturated Fat 6g; Trans Fat 1g); Cholesterol 25mg; Sodium 240mg; Total Carbohydrate 47g (Dietary Fiber 0g); Protein 3g EXCHANGES: 1 Starch, 2 Other Carbohydrate, 3 Fat CARBOHYDRATE CHOICES: 3

sweet note To make the white chocolate–dipped strawberries, melt 4 ounces chopped vanilla candy coating and 1 teaspoon vegetable oil. Dip strawberries in melted coating and place on waxed paper to set.

lemon-ginger bundt cake

prep time: **25 minutes** *start to finish:* **2 hours 20 minutes** [16 SERVINGS]

cake

1 box (1 lb 2.25 oz) Betty Crocker SuperMoist lemon cake mix

¾ cup water

½ cup vegetable oil

½ cup sour cream

1 teaspoon ground ginger

3 eggs

½ cup finely chopped crystallized ginger (about 2½ oz)

frosting

1 cup powdered sugar

½ teaspoon grated fresh lemon peel

4 teaspoons fresh lemon juice

1 Heat oven to 350°F (325°F for dark or nonstick pan). Generously spray 12-cup fluted tube cake pan with baking spray with flour.

2 In medium bowl, beat cake mix, water, oil, sour cream, ground ginger and eggs with electric mixer on low speed 30 seconds. Beat on medium speed 2 minutes, scraping bowl occasionally. Stir crystallized ginger into batter. Pour into pan.

3 Bake 40 to 45 minutes or until toothpick inserted in center comes out clean. Cool 10 minutes. Place cooling rack or heatproof serving plate upside down on pan; turn rack and pan over. Remove pan. Cool completely, about 1 hour.

4 In small bowl, stir frosting ingredients until well blended. Spoon over cake. Store loosely covered at room temperature.

1 SERVING: Calories 270; Total Fat 12g (Saturated Fat 3g; Trans Fat 1g); Cholesterol 45mg; Sodium 230mg; Total Carbohydrate 38g (Dietary Fiber 0g); Protein 2g EXCHANGES: ½ Starch, 2 Other Carbohydrate, 2½ Fat CARBOHYDRATE CHOICES: 2½

sweet note Look for the crystallized ginger in clear plastic bags in the produce department. Buying ginger this way is less expensive than buying it in a jar from the spice section and it tastes the same. If you purchase a 3-ounce package, you'll have enough left over to garnish the cake.

cookies 'n cream angel cake

prep time: **15 minutes**   *start to finish:* **3 hours 15 minutes**   [12 SERVINGS]

1 box (1 lb) Betty Crocker white angel food cake mix

1¼ cups cold water

3 reduced-fat chocolate sandwich cookies, finely crushed

1 box (7.2 oz) fluffy white frosting mix

½ cup boiling water

6 reduced-fat chocolate sandwich cookies, cut in half

1 Move oven rack to lowest position (remove other racks). Heat oven to 350°F.

2 In extra-large glass or metal bowl, beat cake mix and cold water with electric mixer on low speed 30 seconds. Beat on medium speed 1 minute. Carefully fold crushed cookies into batter. Pour into ungreased 10-inch angel food (tube) cake pan. (Do not use fluted tube cake pan or 9-inch angel food pan or batter will overflow.)

3 Bake 37 to 47 minutes or until top is dark golden brown and cracks feel very dry and are not sticky. DO NOT UNDERBAKE. Immediately turn pan upside down onto glass bottle until cake is completely cool, about 2 hours.

4 Run knife around edges of cake; remove from pan. Place on serving plate.

5 In small glass or metal bowl, beat frosting mix and boiling water on low speed 30 seconds, scraping bowl constantly. Beat on high speed 5 to 7 minutes, scraping bowl occasionally, until stiff peaks form. Frost cake; garnish with sandwich cookie halves.

1 SERVING: Calories 240; Total Fat 1g (Saturated Fat 0g; Trans Fat 0g); Cholesterol 0mg; Sodium 400mg; Total Carbohydrate 54g (Dietary Fiber 0g); Protein 3g EXCHANGES: 1 Starch, 2½ Other Carbohydrate CARBOHYDRATE CHOICES: 3½

sweet note This cake is just as delicious without the frosting! Simply top each slice with a dollop of whipped topping and a sandwich cookie.

orange cream angel food cake

prep time: **35 minutes**   *start to finish:* **5 hours 25 minutes**   [12 SERVINGS]

cake

1 box (1 lb) Betty Crocker white angel food cake mix

1¼ cups cold water

orange cream

6 egg yolks

1 cup sugar

2 teaspoons cornstarch

⅔ cup orange juice

Pinch salt

¾ cup butter or margarine, cut into pieces

1 cup whipping cream

1 tablespoon grated orange peel

Orange peel twists, if desired

sweet note When frosting this cake, first seal in the crumbs by spreading a thin layer of orange cream around the side of the cake. Then frost the top and go back over the side for complete coverage.

1 Move oven rack to lowest position (remove other racks). Heat oven to 350°F.

2 In extra-large glass or metal bowl, beat cake mix and cold water with electric mixer on low speed 30 seconds. Beat on medium speed 1 minute. Pour into ungreased 10-inch angel food (tube) cake pan. (Do not use fluted tube cake pan or 9-inch angel food pan or batter will overflow.)

3 Bake 37 to 47 minutes or until top is dark golden brown and cracks feel very dry and are not sticky. DO NOT UNDERBAKE. Immediately turn pan upside down onto glass bottle until cake is completely cool, about 2 hours.

4 Meanwhile, in 2-quart saucepan, beat egg yolks, sugar, cornstarch, orange juice and salt with whisk until blended. Add butter; cook 2 to 3 minutes over medium heat, stirring frequently, until boiling. Boil 3 to 5 minutes, stirring constantly, until thickened and mixture coats the back of a spoon. Immediately pour orange mixture (orange curd) through fine-mesh strainer into medium bowl. Cover with plastic wrap, pressing wrap directly onto surface of orange curd. Refrigerate about 1 hour or until completely chilled.

5 In medium bowl, beat whipping cream on high speed until stiff peaks form. Fold whipped cream and grated orange peel into orange curd.

6 Run knife around edges of cake; remove from pan. On serving plate, place cake with browned side down. Cut off top ⅓ of cake, using long, sharp knife; set aside. Scoop out 1-inch-wide and 1-inch-deep tunnel around cake. (Set aside scooped-out cake for another use.) Spoon 1⅓ cups orange cream into tunnel. Replace top of cake to seal filling. Frost top and side of cake with remaining orange cream. Refrigerate at least 2 hours before serving. Garnish with orange peel twists. Store covered in refrigerator.

1 SERVING: Calories 420; Total Fat 21g (Saturated Fat 13g; Trans Fat 0.5g); Cholesterol 160mg; Sodium 410mg; Total Carbohydrate 51g (Dietary Fiber 0g); Protein 5g EXCHANGES: 3½ Other Carbohydrate, ½ High-Fat Meat, 3½ Fat CARBOHYDRATE CHOICES: 3½

strawberry-rhubarb angel cake

prep time: 25 minutes *start to finish:* 3 hours 15 minutes [12 SERVINGS]

cake

1 box (1 lb) Betty Crocker white angel food cake mix

1¼ cups cold water

2 teaspoons grated orange peel

filling

2 cups sliced rhubarb

½ cup sugar

2 tablespoons orange juice

1½ cups sliced strawberries

4 drops red food color, if desired

frosting and garnish

1 container (8 oz) frozen fat-free whipped topping, thawed

½ cup sliced strawberries

1. Move oven rack to lowest position (remove other racks). Heat oven to 350°F.

2. In extra-large glass or metal bowl, beat cake mix, cold water and orange peel with electric mixer on low speed 30 seconds; beat on medium speed 1 minute. Pour into ungreased 10-inch angel food (tube) cake pan. (Do not use fluted tube cake pan or 9-inch angel food pan or batter will overflow.)

3. Bake 37 to 47 minutes or until top is dark golden brown and cracks feel very dry and are not sticky. DO NOT UNDERBAKE. Immediately turn pan upside down onto glass bottle until cake is completely cool, about 2 hours.

4. Meanwhile, in 2-quart saucepan, mix rhubarb, sugar and orange juice. Cook over medium heat 10 minutes, stirring occasionally. Cool 15 minutes. Stir in 1½ cups strawberries. Stir in food color for a deeper red color. Refrigerate about 1 hour.

5. Run knife around edges of cake; remove from pan. Cut cake horizontally to make 3 layers. (Mark side of cake with toothpicks and cut with long, thin knife.) Fill layers with strawberry-rhubarb filling. Frost side and top of cake with whipped topping. Arrange ½ cup strawberries over top of cake. Store covered in refrigerator.

1 SERVING: Calories 220; Total Fat 0g (Saturated Fat 0g; Trans Fat 0g); Cholesterol 0mg; Sodium 330mg; Total Carbohydrate 50g (Dietary Fiber 1g); Protein 3g EXCHANGES: 1 Starch, 2½ Other Carbohydrate CARBOHYDRATE CHOICES: 3

sweet note If fresh rhubarb is out of season, use frozen rhubarb instead. Be sure to thaw and drain well before making the filling.

chapter three

cupcakes

chai latte cupcakes

prep time: **25 minutes**   *start to finish:* **1 hour 50 minutes**   [24 CUPCAKES]

cupcakes

1 box (1 lb 2.25 oz) Betty Crocker SuperMoist French vanilla cake mix

1½ cups water

⅓ cup vegetable oil

3 eggs

1 package (1.1 oz) instant chai tea latte mix (or 3 tablespoons from larger container)

frosting and garnish

4 oz white chocolate baking bars (from 6-oz package), chopped

⅓ cup butter or margarine, softened

4 cups powdered sugar

¼ cup milk

½ teaspoon vanilla

Ground cinnamon, if desired

1 Heat oven to 350°F (325°F for dark or nonstick pans). Place paper baking cup in each of 24 regular-size muffin cups.

2 In large bowl, beat cupcake ingredients with electric mixer on low speed 30 seconds. Beat on medium speed 2 minutes, scraping bowl occasionally. Divide batter evenly among muffin cups (about ⅔ full).

3 Bake 18 to 23 minutes or until toothpick inserted in center comes out clean. Cool 10 minutes; remove from pan to cooling rack. Cool completely, about 1 hour.

4 In medium microwavable bowl, microwave baking bars on High 30 seconds; stir until melted. If necessary, microwave 15 seconds longer or until melted and smooth. Stir in butter until smooth. Add powdered sugar, milk and vanilla; stir until well blended.

5 Frost cupcakes. Sprinkle with cinnamon. Store loosely covered at room temperature.

1 CUPCAKE: Calories 260; Total Fat 10g (Saturated Fat 3.5g; Trans Fat 0.5g); Cholesterol 35mg; Sodium 180mg; Total Carbohydrate 41g (Dietary Fiber 0g); Protein 2g EXCHANGES: ½ Starch, 2 Other Carbohydrate, 2 Fat CARBOHYDRATE CHOICES: 3

sweet note *Chai* is the Hindi word for a tea made with milk and a variety of spices such as cardamom, cinnamon, cloves, ginger, nutmeg and pepper.

pb & j cupcakes

prep time: 30 minutes *start to finish:* 1 hour 40 minutes [24 CUPCAKES]

cupcakes

1 box (1 lb 2.25 oz) Betty Crocker SuperMoist yellow cake mix

1¼ cups water

¾ cup creamy peanut butter

¼ cup vegetable oil

3 eggs

frosting

1 container (12 oz) vanilla whipped ready-to-spread frosting

½ cup creamy peanut butter

2 to 4 tablespoons grape jelly

1 Heat oven to 350°F (325°F for dark or nonstick pans). Place paper baking cup in each of 24 regular-size muffin cups.

2 In large bowl, beat cupcake ingredients with electric mixer on low speed 30 seconds. Beat on medium speed 2 minutes, scraping bowl occasionally. Divide batter evenly among muffin cups (about ⅔ full).

3 Bake 20 to 25 minutes or until toothpick inserted in center comes out clean. Cool 10 minutes; remove from pan to cooling rack. Cool completely, about 30 minutes.

4 In medium bowl, mix frosting and ½ cup peanut butter. Spread frosting over cupcakes. Make a small indentation in center of frosting on each cupcake with back of spoon. Just before serving, spoon ¼ to ½ teaspoon jelly into each indentation. Store loosely covered at room temperature.

1 CUPCAKE: Calories 270; Total Fat 15g (Saturated Fat 3.5g; Trans Fat 1.5g); Cholesterol 25mg; Sodium 230mg; Total Carbohydrate 30g (Dietary Fiber 0g); Protein 5g EXCHANGES: 1 Starch, 1 Other Carbohydrate, 3 Fat CARBOHYDRATE CHOICES: 2

sweet note No grape jelly on the shelf? Substitute your favorite flavor of jam, preserves or jelly. Jelly or jam in a squeezable container is convenient and makes quick work of topping the cupcakes.

dip-and-twist frosting

Here's a way to quickly and easily frost cupcakes.
Dip the tops into frosting, give a slight twist and remove. Finish off the top with a swirl of a knife. If you are adding toppings, simply swirl or dip the frosting into the desired topper.

strawberry–cream cheese cupcakes

prep time: 20 minutes   *start to finish:* 1 hour 25 minutes   [24 CUPCAKES]

1 box (1 lb 2.25 oz) Betty Crocker SuperMoist yellow cake mix

1 container (8 oz) sour cream

½ cup vegetable oil

½ cup water

2 eggs

3 tablespoons strawberry preserves

1 package (3 oz) cream cheese, cut into 24 pieces

1 container (1 lb) cream cheese creamy ready-to-spread frosting

Sliced fresh small strawberries, if desired

1 Heat oven to 350°F (325°F for dark or nonstick pans). Place paper baking cup in each of 24 regular-size muffin cups.

2 In large bowl, mix cake mix, sour cream, oil, water and eggs with spoon until well blended (batter will be thick). Divide batter evenly among muffin cups (about ⅔ full).

3 In small bowl, stir preserves until smooth. Place 1 piece of cream cheese on top of each cupcake; press into batter slightly. Spoon ¼ measuring teaspoon preserves on top of cream cheese in each cupcake.

4 Bake 18 to 23 minutes or until tops are golden brown and spring back when lightly touched in center (some preserves may show in tops of cupcakes). Cool 10 minutes; remove from pan to cooling rack. Cool completely, about 30 minutes.

5 Frost cupcakes with frosting. Just before serving, garnish each cupcake with strawberry slices. Store covered in refrigerator.

1 CUPCAKE: Calories 260; Total Fat 14g (Saturated Fat 4.5g; Trans Fat 2g); Cholesterol 30mg; Sodium 210mg; Total Carbohydrate 31g (Dietary Fiber 0g); Protein 2g EXCHANGES: ½ Starch, 1½ Other Carbohydrate, 3 Fat CARBOHYDRATE CHOICES: 2

sweet note Turn these tasty treasures into yummy raspberry cupcakes. Just substitute raspberry preserves for the strawberry preserves and garnish with fresh raspberries.

spiced pumpkin cupcakes

prep time: **40 minutes**   *start to finish:* **1 hour 45 minutes**   [24 CUPCAKES]

½ cup finely chopped pecans

3 tablespoons sugar

1 box (1 lb 2.25 oz) Betty Crocker SuperMoist yellow cake mix

1 cup (from 15-oz can) pumpkin (not pumpkin pie mix)

½ cup water

⅓ cup vegetable oil

4 eggs

1½ teaspoons pumpkin pie spice

1 container (1 lb) cream cheese creamy ready-to-spread frosting

1 Heat oven to 350°F (325°F for dark or nonstick pans). Place paper baking cup in each of 24 regular-size muffin cups.

2 In 8-inch nonstick skillet, cook pecans and 2 tablespoons of the sugar over low heat about 8 minutes, stirring frequently, until sugar is melted. Spoon and spread pecans onto sheet of waxed paper. Sprinkle with remaining 1 tablespoon sugar; toss.

3 In large bowl, beat cake mix, pumpkin, water, oil, eggs and pumpkin pie spice with electric mixer on low speed 30 seconds. Beat on medium speed 2 minutes, scraping bowl occasionally. Divide batter evenly among muffin cups (about ⅔ full).

4 Bake 20 to 25 minutes or until toothpick inserted in center comes out clean. Cool 10 minutes; remove from pan to cooling rack. Cool completely, about 30 minutes.

5 Frost cupcakes with frosting. Sprinkle edge of frosted cupcakes with pecans; press lightly into frosting.

1 CUPCAKE: Calories 230; Total Fat 10g (Saturated Fat 2g; Trans Fat 1.5g); Cholesterol 35mg; Sodium 210mg; Total Carbohydrate 34g (Dietary Fiber 0g); Protein 2g EXCHANGES: 1 Starch, 1 Other Carbohydrate, 2 Fat CARBOHYDRATE CHOICES: 2

sweet note These are great cupcakes for a snack or party. For a special occasion, serve them arranged on a pretty platter surrounded with fresh fruit.

mr. sun cupcakes

prep time: **1 hour 15 minutes**   *start to finish:* **2 hours 20 minutes**   [24 CUPCAKES]

cupcakes

1 box (1 lb 2.25 oz) Betty Crocker SuperMoist yellow cake mix

Water, vegetable oil and eggs called for on cake mix box

frosting and decorations

Yellow food color

1 container (1 lb) vanilla creamy ready-to-spread frosting

Powdered sugar

48 large yellow, orange and/or red gumdrops

Black decorating icing (from 4.25-oz tube)

Red decorating gel (from 0.68-oz tube)

1 Heat oven to 350°F (325°F for dark or nonstick pans). Place paper baking cup in each of 24 regular-size muffin cups.

2 Make cake mix as directed on box, using water, oil and egg whites. Divide batter evenly among muffin cups (about ⅔ full).

3 Bake as directed on box or until toothpick inserted in center comes out clean. Cool 10 minutes; remove from pan to cooling rack. Cool completely, about 30 minutes.

4 Stir 15 drops food color into frosting until bright yellow. Frost cupcakes.

5 Lightly sprinkle powdered sugar on work surface and rolling pin. Roll 4 gumdrops at a time into flat ovals about ⅛ inch thick. Cut thin sliver off top and bottom of each oval to make rectangles. Cut each rectangle in half crosswise to make 2 squares; cut each square diagonally in half to make 2 triangles.

6 Arrange 8 gumdrop triangles around edge of each cupcake for sun rays. Using small writing tip on black icing tube, pipe sunglasses onto each cupcake. Using red gel, pipe smiling mouth onto each cupcake. Refrigerate until ready to serve. Store covered in refrigerator.

1 FROSTED CUPCAKE (UNDECORATED): Calories 200; Total Fat 8g (Saturated Fat 2g; Trans Fat 1.5g); Cholesterol 25mg; Sodium 190mg; Total Carbohydrate 30g (Dietary Fiber 0g); Protein 1g EXCHANGES: 2 Other Carbohydrate, 1½ Fat CARBOHYDRATE CHOICES: 2

sweet note Roll and cut the sun rays ahead of time so kids can help assemble the cupcakes. If you want brighter yellow frosting, try using gel food color instead of liquid.

hot chocolate cupcakes

prep time: 20 minutes   *start to finish:* 1 hour 25 minutes   [12 CUPCAKES]

1¾ cups Betty Crocker SuperMoist devil's food cake mix (from 1 lb 2.25-oz box)

½ cup water

3 tablespoons vegetable oil

1 egg

1 cup vanilla whipped ready-to-spread frosting (from 12-oz container)

½ cup marshmallow creme

¼ teaspoon unsweetened baking cocoa

6 miniature pretzel twists, broken in half

1 Heat oven to 350°F (325°F for dark or nonstick pan). Place paper baking cup in each of 12 regular-size muffin cups.

2 In large bowl, beat cake mix, water, oil and egg with electric mixer on low speed 30 seconds. Beat on medium speed 2 minutes, scraping bowl occasionally. Divide batter evenly among muffin cups (about ⅔ full).

3 Bake 17 to 22 minutes or until toothpick inserted in center comes out clean. Cool 10 minutes; remove from pan to cooling rack. Cool completely, about 30 minutes.

4 In small bowl, mix frosting and marshmallow creme. Spoon into resealable food-storage plastic bag; seal bag. Cut tiny hole in one corner of bag. (Or spoon mixture onto cupcakes instead of piping.)

5 Pipe 3 small dollops of frosting mixture on top of each cupcake to resemble melted marshmallows. Sprinkle with cocoa. Press pretzel half into side of each cupcake for cup handle.

1 CUPCAKE: Calories 240; Total Fat 9g (Saturated Fat 2.5g; Trans Fat 1.5g); Cholesterol 20mg; Sodium 300mg; Total Carbohydrate 37g (Dietary Fiber 0g); Protein 2g EXCHANGES: 2½ Other Carbohydrate, 2 Fat CARBOHYDRATE CHOICES: 2½

sweet note If you are making these around the holidays and are feeling festive, sprinkle the frosted cupcakes with crushed peppermint candy canes.

red velvet cupcakes with cream cheese frosting

prep time: **20 minutes**   *start to finish:* **1 hour 25 minutes**   [24 CUPCAKES]

1 teaspoon water

1 bottle (1 oz) red food color

1 box (1 lb 2.25 oz) Betty Crocker SuperMoist devil's food cake mix

1¼ cups water

½ cup vegetable oil

3 eggs

1 container (1 lb) cream cheese creamy ready-to-spread frosting

1 Heat oven to 375°F (350°F for dark or nonstick pans). Place paper baking cup in each of 24 regular-size muffin cups.

2 In small bowl, mix 1 teaspoon water and 3 or 4 drops of the food color; set aside.

3 In large bowl, beat cake mix, 1¼ cups water, the oil, eggs and remaining food color with electric mixer on low speed 30 seconds. Beat on medium speed 2 minutes, scraping bowl occasionally. Divide batter evenly among muffin cups (about ⅔ full).

4 Bake 18 to 23 minutes or until toothpick inserted in center comes out clean. Cool 10 minutes; remove from pan to cooling rack. Cool completely, about 30 minutes.

5 Frost cupcakes with frosting. Using a fine-tip brush, paint cupcakes with red food color "paint," swirling to create design. Store loosely covered at room temperature.

1 CUPCAKE: Calories 220; Total Fat 11g (Saturated Fat 3g; Trans Fat 0g); Cholesterol 25mg; Sodium 220mg; Total Carbohydrate 29g (Dietary Fiber 0g); Protein 2g EXCHANGES: 1 Starch, 1 Other Carbohydrate, 2 Fat CARBOHYDRATE CHOICES: 2

sweet note Serve these pretty cupcakes with vanilla ice cream topped with red candy sprinkles or a drizzle of grenadine syrup.

cake mix

teddy-at-the-beach cupcakes

prep time: 30 minutes   *start to finish:* 1 hour 35 minutes   [12 CUPCAKES]

1 box Betty Crocker
SuperMoist cake mix
(any flavor)

Water, vegetable oil and
eggs called for on cake
mix box

2 drops blue food color

1 cup vanilla whipped
ready-to-spread frosting
(from 12-oz container)

1 roll (from 4.5-oz box)
chewy fruit-flavored
snack (any flavor)

½ cup teddy bear–shaped
graham snacks, crushed,
or brown sugar

1 tablespoon blue sugar or
edible glitter, if desired

12 teddy bear–shaped
graham snacks

6 paper drink umbrellas or
small plastic umbrellas,
if desired

6 ring-shaped gummy
candies

6 multi-colored fish-shaped
crackers

1 Heat oven to 350°F (325°F for dark or nonstick pans). Place paper baking cup in each of 24 regular-size muffin cups.

2 Make cake mix as directed on box, using water, oil and eggs. Divide batter evenly among muffin cups (about ⅔ full).

3 Bake as directed on box or until toothpick inserted in center comes out clean. Cool 10 minutes; remove from pan to cooling rack. Cool completely, about 30 minutes.

4 Tightly wrap 12 cupcakes; freeze for a later use. Stir blue food color into frosting until blended. Frost remaining 12 cupcakes.

5 Cut 6 (1½-inch) pieces from fruit snack roll; peel off paper backing. Use fruit snack, crushed graham snacks, blue sugar, teddy bear–shaped snacks, umbrellas, gummy candies and fish-shaped crackers to decorate cupcakes as shown in photo or as desired.

1 FROSTED CUPCAKE (UNDECORATED): Calories 190; Total Fat 9g (Saturated Fat 2.5g; Trans Fat 1.5g); Cholesterol 25mg; Sodium 160mg; Total Carbohydrate 28g (Dietary Fiber 0g); Protein 1g EXCHANGES: ½ Starch, 1½ Other Carbohydrate, 1½ Fat CARBOHYDRATE CHOICES: 2

sweet note Add swim suits to the bears on top of the cupcakes with decorating icing that comes in a tube. Look for the plastic umbrellas at www.fancyflours.com.

happy birthday marshmallow cupcakes

prep time: 25 minutes   *start to finish:* 1 hour 25 minutes   [24 CUPCAKES]

1 box (1 lb 2.25 oz) Betty Crocker SuperMoist white cake mix

Water, vegetable oil and egg whites called for on cake mix box

2 containers (1 lb each) creamy white ready-to-spread frosting

24 to 30 large marshmallows

Colored sugar or candy sprinkles

White or colored birthday candles

1 Heat oven to 350°F (325°F for dark or nonstick pans). Place paper baking cup in each of 24 regular-size muffin cups.

2 Make cake mix as directed on box, using water, oil and egg whites. Divide batter evenly among muffin cups (about ⅔ full).

3 Bake as directed on box or until toothpick inserted in center comes out clean. Cool 10 minutes; remove from pan to cooling rack. Cool completely, about 30 minutes.

4 Frost cupcakes with frosting. With dampened kitchen scissors, cut marshmallows into slices; sprinkle with colored sugar. Arrange on cupcakes in flower shape. Place candle in middle of each flower.

1 CUPCAKE: Calories 280; Total Fat 14g (Saturated Fat 4g; Trans Fat 3g); Cholesterol 0mg; Sodium 240mg; Total Carbohydrate 38g (Dietary Fiber 0g); Protein 1g EXCHANGES: 2½ Other Carbohydrate, 3 Fat CARBOHYDRATE CHOICES: 2½

freezing cupcakes

Unfrosted cupcakes freeze best. Plan to frost them when you remove them from the freezer.

- **Cool cupcakes** 30 minutes before covering and freezing.

- **Freeze in tightly covered container** for up to 3 months.

- **Frost cupcakes frozen** or thaw at room temperature and then frost.

- **If you do freeze them frosted** (creamy frosting works best), freeze uncovered for 1 hour, then cover tightly.

sweet note There's a variety of unique, really fun birthday candles available at party-supply or cake-decorating stores. It's a great way to personalize your cupcakes. Also, edible glitter instead of the colored sugar is a clever way to add sparkle to the cupcakes.

toasted almond cupcakes with caramel frosting

prep time: **25 minutes**   *start to finish:* **2 hours**   [24 CUPCAKES]

cupcakes

1½ cups sliced almonds

1 box (1 lb 2.25 oz) Betty Crocker SuperMoist white cake mix

1¼ cups water

⅓ cup vegetable oil

1 teaspoon almond extract

3 eggs

caramel frosting

½ cup butter or margarine

1 cup packed brown sugar

¼ cup milk

2 cups powdered sugar

1 Heat oven to 350°F (325°F for dark or nonstick pans). Place paper baking cup in each of 24 regular-size muffin cups.

2 In shallow pan, bake almonds 6 to 10 minutes, stirring occasionally, until golden brown. Cool 15 minutes. Reserve 1 cup almonds for garnish. In food processor, process remaining almonds until finely ground.

3 In large bowl, beat cake mix, water, oil, almond extract and eggs with electric mixer on low speed 30 seconds. Beat on medium speed 2 minutes, scraping bowl occasionally (batter will be lumpy). Fold in ground almonds. Divide batter evenly among muffin cups (about ⅔ full).

4 Bake 15 to 20 minutes or until toothpick inserted in center comes out clean. Cool 10 minutes; remove from pan to cooling rack. Cool completely, about 30 minutes.

5 Meanwhile, in 2-quart saucepan, melt butter over medium heat. Stir in brown sugar. Heat to boiling, stirring constantly. Reduce heat to low; boil and stir 2 minutes. Stir in milk. Heat to boiling. Remove from heat. Cool to lukewarm, about 30 minutes.

6 Gradually stir powdered sugar into brown sugar mixture. Place saucepan of frosting in bowl of cold water. Beat with spoon until smooth and spreadable. If frosting becomes too stiff, stir in additional milk, 1 teaspoon at a time.

7 Frost a few cupcakes at a time with 1 tablespoon frosting each; press reserved almonds lightly into frosting. Store loosely covered at room temperature.

sweet note These pretty cupcakes are ideal for a bake sale. Package them in boxes of six and tie each box with decorative ribbon.

1 CUPCAKE: Calories 270; Total Fat 13g (Saturated Fat 4g; Trans Fat 0.5g); Cholesterol 35mg; Sodium 190mg; Total Carbohydrate 37g (Dietary Fiber 0g); Protein 3g EXCHANGES: ½ Starch, 2 Other Carbohydrate, 2½ Fat CARBOHYDRATE CHOICES: 2½

lemon cupcakes with strawberry frosting

prep time: **40 minutes**   *start to finish:* **1 hour 45 minutes**   [24 CUPCAKES]

cupcakes

1 box (1 lb 2.25 oz) Betty Crocker SuperMoist white cake mix

Water, vegetable oil and egg whites called for on cake mix box

3 tablespoons grated lemon peel

frosting

4 to 6 medium strawberries (about 4 oz), hulled

1 container (12 oz) fluffy white whipped ready-to-spread frosting

garnish, if desired

12 strawberries, sliced

Lemon peel curls

1 Heat oven to 350°F (325°F for dark or nonstick pans). Place paper baking cup in each of 24 regular-size muffin cups.

2 Make cake mix as directed on box, using water, oil and egg whites and adding grated lemon peel. Divide batter evenly among muffin cups (about ⅔ full).

3 Bake as directed on box or until toothpick inserted in center comes out clean. Cool 10 minutes; remove from pan to cooling rack. Cool completely, about 30 minutes.

4 Place whole strawberries in blender. Cover; pulse 20 seconds to puree. Pour ¼ cup of the strawberry puree into medium bowl. Stir in frosting until well mixed.

5 Frost cupcakes. Garnish with sliced strawberries and lemon peel curls.

1 CUPCAKE: Calories 180; Total Fat 7g (Saturated Fat 2g; Trans Fat 1.5g); Cholesterol 0mg; Sodium 160mg; Total Carbohydrate 26g (Dietary Fiber 0g); Protein 1g EXCHANGES: 1½ Other Carbohydrate, 1½ Fat CARBOHYDRATE CHOICES: 2

sweet note Here's an easy way to hull strawberries. Push one end of a plastic drinking straw into the point of the berry and push it through to pop off the green cap.

chocolate cupcakes with penuche filling

prep time: **40 minutes**   *start to finish:* **2 hours 10 minutes**   [24 CUPCAKES]

cupcakes

1 box (1 lb 2.25 oz) Betty Crocker SuperMoist chocolate fudge cake mix

1⅓ cups water

½ cup vegetable oil

3 eggs

1 teaspoon vanilla

filling and garnish

1 cup butter or margarine

2 cups packed brown sugar

½ cup milk

4 cups powdered sugar

1 oz grated semisweet baking chocolate, if desired

sweet note The word *penuche* comes from a Spanish word meaning "raw sugar" or "brown sugar." It is used to describe a fudgelike candy made from brown sugar, butter, milk or cream, and vanilla.

1 Heat oven to 350°F (325°F for dark or nonstick pans). Place paper baking cup in each of 24 regular-size muffin cups. Spray bottom of each paper cup with baking spray with flour.

2 In large bowl, beat cake mix, water, oil, eggs and vanilla with electric mixer on low speed 30 seconds. Beat on medium speed 2 minutes, scraping bowl occasionally. Divide batter evenly among muffin cups.

3 Bake 18 to 24 minutes or until toothpick inserted in center comes out clean. Cool 15 minutes; remove from pan to cooling rack. Cool completely, about 30 minutes.

4 Meanwhile, in 2-quart saucepan, melt butter over medium heat. Stir in brown sugar. Heat to boiling, stirring constantly; reduce heat to low. Boil and stir 2 minutes. Stir in milk. Heat to boiling; remove from heat. Pour mixture into medium bowl; refrigerate about 30 minutes or until lukewarm.

5 Beat powdered sugar into cooled brown sugar mixture on low speed until smooth. If frosting becomes too stiff, stir in additional milk, 1 teaspoon at a time.

6 Using serrated knife, cut each cupcake in half horizontally, being careful not to break either half. Place 1 heaping tablespoon filling on each cupcake base. Replace rounded cupcake tops. Pipe or spoon rounded 1 tablespoon frosting onto cupcake tops. Garnish with grated chocolate. Store in airtight container at room temperature.

1 CUPCAKE: Calories 360; Total Fat 15g (Saturated Fat 6g; Trans Fat 0.5g); Cholesterol 45mg; Sodium 240mg; Total Carbohydrate 56g (Dietary Fiber 0g); Protein 2g EXCHANGES: ½ Starch, 3 Other Carbohydrate, 3 Fat CARBOHYDRATE CHOICES: 4

wedding cupcakes

prep time: 1 hour   *start to finish:* 2 hours 25 minutes   [24 CUPCAKES]

cupcakes

1 box (1 lb 2.25 oz) Betty Crocker SuperMoist white cake mix

Water, vegetable oil and egg whites called for on cake mix box

2 containers (1 lb each) creamy white ready-to-spread frosting

decorating options

White Chocolate Curls

Pink rose petals

Specialty paper, cut into 8 × 1¼-inch strips

sweet note Look for edible flowers and/or rose petals in the produce department of the grocery store. Edible flowers have not been treated with chemicals, so they're safe to eat.

1 Heat oven to 350°F (325°F for dark or nonstick pans). Place paper baking cup in each of 24 regular-size muffin cups.

2 Make cake mix as directed on box, using water, oil and egg whites. Divide batter evenly among muffin cups (about ⅔ full).

3 Bake as directed on box or until toothpick inserted in center comes out clean. Cool 10 minutes; remove from pan to cooling rack. Cool completely, about 30 minutes.

4 Frost cupcakes with frosting. Choose from these decorating options:

- Top cupcakes with White Chocolate Curls (see below) or rose petals.

- Wrap specialty paper around each cupcake; attach with permanent double-stick tape.

1 FROSTED CUPCAKE (UNDECORATED): Calories 270; Total Fat 11g (Saturated Fat 2.5g; Trans Fat 2.5g); Cholesterol 25mg; Sodium 230mg; Total Carbohydrate 42g (Dietary Fiber 0g); Protein 1g EXCHANGES: 3 Other Carbohydrate, 2 Fat CARBOHYDRATE CHOICES: 3

white chocolate curls: Place a bar of room-temperature white chocolate on waxed paper. Make curls by pulling a vegetable peeler toward you in long, thin strokes while pressing firmly against the chocolate. (If curls crumble or stay too straight, chocolate may be too cold; placing the heel of your hand on the chocolate will warm it enough to get good curls.) Transfer each curl carefully with a toothpick directly onto a frosted cupcake or to a waxed paper–lined cookie sheet.

key lime cupcakes

prep time: 30 minutes   *start to finish:* 1 hour 35 minutes   [24 CUPCAKES]

cupcakes

1 box (1 lb 2.25 oz) Betty Crocker SuperMoist lemon cake mix

1 box (4-serving size) lime-flavored gelatin

¾ cup water

⅓ cup Key lime juice

⅓ cup vegetable oil

3 eggs

2 or 3 drops green food color, if desired

glaze

1 cup powdered sugar

2 to 2½ tablespoons Key lime juice

frosting

1 package (8 oz) cream cheese, softened

¼ cup butter or margarine, softened

1 teaspoon vanilla

3½ cups powdered sugar

Grated lime peel, if desired

1 Heat oven to 350°F (325°F for dark or nonstick pans). Place paper baking cup in each of 24 regular-size muffin cups.

2 In large bowl, beat cake mix and gelatin with electric mixer on low speed 30 seconds. Add remaining cupcake ingredients. Beat with electric mixer on low speed 30 seconds; beat on medium speed 2 minutes, scraping bowl occasionally. Divide batter evenly among muffin cups (about ⅔ full).

3 Bake 17 to 22 minutes or until toothpick inserted in center comes out clean. Cool 10 minutes; remove from pan to cooling rack. With toothpick or wooden skewer, pierce tops of cupcakes in several places.

4 In small bowl, mix 1 cup powdered sugar and enough of the lime juice until glaze is smooth and thin enough to drizzle. Drizzle and spread glaze over cupcakes. Cool completely, about 30 minutes.

5 In large bowl, beat cream cheese and butter on medium speed until light and fluffy. On low speed, beat in vanilla and 3½ cups powdered sugar until mixed; beat on medium speed until fluffy.

6 Frost cupcakes, mounding and swirling frosting in center. Garnish with lime peel. Store covered in refrigerator.

1 CUPCAKE: Calories 280; Total Fat 10g (Saturated Fat 4.5g; Trans Fat 0.5g); Cholesterol 40mg; Sodium 210mg; Total Carbohydrate 43g (Dietary Fiber 0g); Protein 2g EXCHANGES: ½ Starch, 2½ Other Carbohydrate, 2 Fat CARBOHYDRATE CHOICES: 3

sweet note Garnish each cupcake with a small piece of jellied lime candy slice instead of the lime peel.

lemon-blueberry cupcakes

prep time: 25 minutes *start to finish:* 2 hours [24 CUPCAKES]

cupcakes

1 box (1 lb 2.25 oz) Betty Crocker SuperMoist lemon cake mix

¾ cup water

⅓ cup vegetable oil

1 tablespoon grated lemon peel

2 eggs

1 package (3 oz) cream cheese, softened

1½ cups fresh blueberries

frosting and garnish

2½ cups powdered sugar

¾ cup unsalted butter, softened

1 teaspoon grated lemon peel

½ teaspoon kosher (coarse) salt

1¼ teaspoons vanilla

1 tablespoon milk

1 cup fresh blueberries

Lemon peel twists, if desired

Fresh mint leaves, if desired

1 Heat oven to 375°F (350°F for dark or nonstick pans). Place paper baking cup in each of 24 regular-size muffin cups.

2 In large bowl, beat all cupcake ingredients except blueberries with electric mixer on low speed 30 seconds. Beat on medium speed 2 minutes, scraping bowl occasionally. Fold in 1½ cups blueberries. Divide batter evenly among muffin cups (about ⅔ full).

3 Bake 18 to 22 minutes or until tops are light golden brown. Cool 10 minutes; remove from pan to cooling rack. Cool completely, about 1 hour.

4 In medium bowl, beat powdered sugar, butter, grated lemon peel, salt, vanilla and milk on high speed about 4 minutes or until smooth and well blended, adding more milk 1 teaspoon at a time if needed.

5 Frost cupcakes. Garnish with 1 cup blueberries, lemon peel twists and mint leaves. Store in airtight container at room temperature.

1 CUPCAKE: Calories 250; Total Fat 12g (Saturated Fat 6g; Trans Fat 1g); Cholesterol 35mg; Sodium 210mg; Total Carbohydrate 32g (Dietary Fiber 0g); Protein 2g EXCHANGES: ½ Starch, 1½ Other Carbohydrate, 2½ Fat CARBOHYDRATE CHOICES: 2

sweet note Unsalted butter tastes a little sweeter than regular salted butter. The kosher salt adds small bursts of saltiness to complement the sweetness of the other ingredients and brings out the lemon flavor. If you don't have unsalted butter, you can use salted butter and omit the kosher salt.

chapter four

page
118

page
144

page
150

cookies & bars

crisp chocolate-espresso ribbon cookies

prep time: **30 minutes**   *start to finish:* **3 hours 10 minutes**   [4 DOZEN COOKIES]

1 pouch (1 lb 1.5 oz) Betty Crocker sugar cookie mix

1 tablespoon all-purpose flour

½ cup butter or margarine, softened

1 teaspoon almond extract

1 egg, slightly beaten

⅓ cup bittersweet chocolate chips, melted

½ cup coarsely to finely crushed chocolate-covered espresso coffee beans

⅓ cup coarsely chopped toasted almonds

sweet note The chocolate-covered espresso coffee beans add a lot of flavor to these crisp cookies. You'll find them at your favorite coffee shop or by the coffee in the grocery store.

1 Line bottom and sides of 9 × 5-inch loaf pan with plastic wrap.

2 In large bowl, stir cookie mix, flour, butter, almond extract and egg until soft dough forms. Divide dough in half; place half of dough in another bowl. Stir melted chocolate into half of dough. To remaining half of dough, mix in espresso beans and almonds.

3 Firmly press half of chocolate dough evenly in bottom of loaf pan. Evenly press half of espresso dough over chocolate dough in pan. Repeat with remaining chocolate dough and espresso dough. Fold plastic wrap over dough to cover. Refrigerate until firm, about 2 hours.

4 Heat oven to 350°F. Remove dough from pan; unwrap. Place dough on cutting board. Cut dough crosswise into 4 equal pieces. Cut each piece crosswise into 12 slices. On ungreased cookie sheets, place slices 2 inches apart.

5 Bake 9 to 10 minutes or until edges are light golden brown. Cool 1 minute; remove from cookie sheets to cooling racks.

1 COOKIE: Calories 80; Total Fat 4.5g (Saturated Fat 2g; Trans Fat 0g); Cholesterol 10mg; Sodium 45mg; Total Carbohydrate 10g (Dietary Fiber 0g); Protein 1g EXCHANGES: ½ Starch, 1 Fat CARBOHYDRATE CHOICES: ½

softening butter

When a recipe calls for softened butter, let it stand at room temperature for 30 to 45 minutes. Perfectly softened butter should give gently to pressure, but it shouldn't be soft in appearance and will still hold the stick shape.

aloha paradise bars

prep time: 25 minutes   *start to finish:* 1 hour 15 minutes   [36 BARS]

1 pouch (1 lb 1.5 oz) Betty
Crocker sugar cookie
mix

½ cup butter or margarine,
softened

1 egg

1 bag (12 oz) white vanilla
baking chips (2 cups)

1 cup coarsely chopped
dried pineapple

1 cup flaked coconut

1 cup chopped macadamia
nuts

1 can (14 oz) sweetened
condensed milk
(not evaporated)

1 Heat oven to 350°F. Spray bottom only of 13 × 9-inch pan with
cooking spray.

2 In large bowl, stir cookie mix, butter and egg until soft dough forms.
Press dough in bottom of pan using floured fingers.

3 Bake 15 minutes. Sprinkle with baking chips, pineapple, coconut and
nuts. Drizzle evenly with condensed milk. Bake 30 to 35 minutes
longer or until light golden brown. Cool completely, about 30 minutes.

4 For bars, cut into 9 rows by 4 rows. Store covered in refrigerator.

1 BAR: Calories 230; Total Fat 12g (Saturated Fat 6g; Trans Fat 0.5g); Cholesterol 15mg;
Sodium 100mg; Total Carbohydrate 29g (Dietary Fiber 0g); Protein 3g EXCHANGES: 1 Starch,
1 Other Carbohydrate, 2 Fat CARBOHYDRATE CHOICES: 2

sweet note The macadamia nuts are scrumptious
in these rich bars, but pecans or walnuts would be just
as delicious.

cran-orange 'n date-nut cookies

prep time: 1 hour *start to finish:* 1 hour [ABOUT 3½ DOZEN COOKIES]

⅓ cup dried cranberries

¼ cup chopped orange slice candies

¼ cup coarsely chopped dates

2 tablespoons fresh orange juice

1 pouch (1 lb 1.5 oz) Betty Crocker sugar cookie mix

2 tablespoons all-purpose flour

½ teaspoon ground cinnamon

¼ teaspoon ground ginger

⅓ cup butter or margarine, melted

1 teaspoon grated orange peel

1 egg

1 cup chopped pistachio nuts

½ cup flaked coconut

1 Heat oven to 375°F.

2 In small bowl, mix cranberries, candies, dates and orange juice; set aside. In large bowl, stir cookie mix, flour, cinnamon and ginger until blended. Stir in butter, orange peel and egg until soft dough forms. Stir in cranberry mixture, nuts and coconut until thoroughly mixed.

3 Onto ungreased cookie sheets, drop dough by teaspoonfuls 2 inches apart.

4 Bake 10 to 12 minutes or until edges are light golden brown. Cool 5 minutes; remove from cookie sheets to cooling racks. Store cooled cookies tightly covered.

1 COOKIE: Calories 100; Total Fat 4.5g (Saturated Fat 1.5g; Trans Fat 0.5g); Cholesterol 10mg; Sodium 45mg; Total Carbohydrate 15g (Dietary Fiber 0g); Protein 1g EXCHANGES: ½ Starch, ½ Other Carbohydrate, 1 Fat CARBOHYDRATE CHOICES: 1

evenly sized cookies

Use a spring-loaded scoop to make cookies that are all the same size, so they'll bake evenly and for the same time. Look for the cookie scoops at kitchen specialty stores.

sweet note Remember to grate the peel from the orange before squeezing the juice for these cookies.

lemon linzer bars

prep time: 20 minutes   *start to finish:* 5 hours 15 minutes   [24 BARS]

cookie base

1 pouch (1 lb 1.5 oz) Betty Crocker sugar cookie mix

⅓ cup butter or margarine, softened

2 oz cream cheese, softened

4½ teaspoons frozen (thawed) lemonade concentrate

¾ teaspoon almond extract

1 egg

filling

⅔ cup seedless raspberry jam

1 package (8 oz) cream cheese, softened

½ cup lemon curd (from 10- to 12-oz jar)

2 cups frozen (thawed) whipped topping or 2 cups sweetened whipped cream

topping

⅓ cup sliced almonds, toasted*

24 fresh or frozen (thawed and drained) raspberries

1 Heat oven to 350°F. Spray bottom and sides of 13 × 9-inch pan with cooking spray.

2 In large bowl, stir cookie base ingredients until soft dough forms. Spread dough in bottom of pan.

3 Bake 20 to 23 minutes or until golden brown. Cool completely, about 30 minutes.

4 Spread raspberry jam over cooled base. In large bowl, beat cream cheese and lemon curd with electric mixer on medium speed until smooth. Fold in whipped topping. Drop lemon mixture by teaspoonfuls over jam layer; spread gently and evenly over jam.

5 Sprinkle almonds over top. Refrigerate at least 4 hours or overnight.

6 For bars, cut into 6 rows by 4 rows. To serve, top each bar with 1 raspberry, gently pressing into lemon mixture. Store covered in refrigerator.

* *To toast almonds, bake in ungreased shallow pan in 350°F oven about 10 minutes, stirring occasionally, until golden brown.*

1 BAR: Calories 230; Total Fat 11g (Saturated Fat 6g; Trans Fat 1g); Cholesterol 35mg; Sodium 115mg; Total Carbohydrate 30g (Dietary Fiber 0g); Protein 2g EXCHANGES: 2 Other Carbohydrate, ½ High-Fat Meat, 1½ Fat CARBOHYDRATE CHOICES: 2

sweet note Lemon curd is a lovely, thick, not-too-sweet product that you'll find next to the jams and jellies at the grocery store.

cinna-spin cookies

prep time: 1 hour 10 minutes   *start to finish:* 1 hour 10 minutes   [2½ DOZEN COOKIES]

cookies

1 pouch (1 lb 1.5 oz) Betty Crocker sugar cookie mix

½ teaspoon ground cinnamon

½ cup butter or margarine, softened

1 egg, slightly beaten

1 tablespoon ground cinnamon

glaze

1 cup powdered sugar

2 tablespoons milk

¼ teaspoon vanilla

1. Heat oven to 375°F.

2. In large bowl, mix cookie mix and ½ teaspoon cinnamon. Stir in butter and egg until soft dough forms.

3. On piece of waxed paper, shape 1 tablespoon cinnamon into a line about 5 inches long. Using floured fingers, shape 1 tablespoon of dough into a rope 5 inches long. Press one side of dough rope into cinnamon. Coil dough rope tightly, cinnamon side facing center, into cinnamon-roll shape. Press end of rope into roll to seal.

4. Repeat with remaining dough. Place cookies 2 inches apart on ungreased cookie sheets.

5. Bake 7 to 10 minutes or until edges are light golden brown. Cool 1 minute; remove from cookie sheets to cooling racks. Cool completely, about 15 minutes.

6. In small bowl, mix glaze ingredients until smooth. Drizzle over cookies. Let stand until set.

1 COOKIE: Calories 110; Total Fat 5g (Saturated Fat 2.5g; Trans Fat 0.5g); Cholesterol 15mg; Sodium 70mg; Total Carbohydrate 17g (Dietary Fiber 0g); Protein 1g EXCHANGES: 1 Other Carbohydrate, 1 Fat CARBOHYDRATE CHOICES: 1

sweet note Serve these fun cookies as an after-school snack with a glass of milk.

chocolate-marshmallow pillows

prep time: 45 minutes *start to finish:* 1 hour 10 minutes [2 DOZEN COOKIES]

cookies

1 pouch (1 lb 1.5 oz)
Betty Crocker double
chocolate chunk cookie
mix

¼ cup vegetable oil

2 tablespoons water

1 egg

⅔ cup chopped pecans

12 large marshmallows,
cut in half

frosting

1 cup semisweet chocolate
chips (6 oz)

⅓ cup whipping cream

1 teaspoon butter or
margarine

1 teaspoon vanilla

½ cup powdered sugar

1 Heat oven to 350°F.

2 In large bowl, stir cookie mix, oil, water, egg and pecans until soft dough forms. Onto ungreased cookie sheets, drop dough by rounded tablespoonfuls 2 inches apart.

3 Bake 7 minutes. Remove from oven; immediately press marshmallow half lightly, cut side down, on top of cookie. Bake 1 to 2 minutes longer or just until marshmallows begin to soften. Cool 2 minutes; remove from cookie sheets to cooling racks. Cool completely, about 15 minutes.

4 Meanwhile, in 1-quart nonstick saucepan, melt chocolate chips over low heat, stirring until smooth. Remove from heat. Add whipping cream, butter and vanilla; blend well. Stir in powdered sugar until smooth.

5 Spread frosting over each cooled cookie, covering marshmallow. Let stand until frosting is set.

1 COOKIE: Calories 200; Total Fat 10g (Saturated Fat 3g; Trans Fat 1g); Cholesterol 15mg; Sodium 70mg; Total Carbohydrate 26g (Dietary Fiber 0g); Protein 1g EXCHANGES: ½ Starch, 1 Other Carbohydrate, 2 Fat CARBOHYDRATE CHOICES: 2

sweet note For the best results, always be sure to use marshmallows that are very fresh and soft when baking these or any other cookie treats.

almond, apricot and white chocolate decadence bars

prep time: **35 minutes**   *start to finish:* **3 hours 35 minutes**   [36 BARS]

cookie base

1 pouch (1 lb 1.5 oz) Betty Crocker sugar cookie mix

½ cup butter or margarine, melted

½ teaspoon almond extract

1 egg, slightly beaten

filling

1 package (7 or 8 oz) almond paste (not marzipan)

½ cup sugar

1 cup finely chopped dried apricots (6 oz)

6 oz cream cheese, softened

2 eggs

1 teaspoon lemon juice

topping

1 bag (12 oz) white vanilla baking chips (2 cups)

⅔ cup whipping cream

½ cup sliced almonds

1 Heat oven to 375°F.

2 In large bowl, stir cookie base ingredients until soft dough forms. Spread dough in bottom of ungreased 13 × 9-inch pan.

3 Bake 10 to 15 minutes or until set. Cool 10 minutes.

4 Meanwhile, in large bowl, beat almond paste and sugar with electric mixer on low speed until crumbly but blended. Add apricots; beat on low speed just until combined. Add cream cheese, eggs and lemon juice; beat on medium speed until well blended. Pour over warm cookie base.

5 Bake 20 to 25 minutes longer or until set. Cool 30 minutes.

6 Place baking chips in small bowl. In 1-quart saucepan, heat whipping cream just to boiling over low heat, stirring occasionally; pour over baking chips. Let stand 1 minute. Stir until chips are melted and mixture is smooth. Pour and spread over filling. Sprinkle with almonds. Refrigerate until set, about 2 hours.

7 For bars, cut into 9 rows by 4 rows. Store covered in refrigerator.

1 BAR: Calories 220; Total Fat 12g (Saturated Fat 6g; Trans Fat 0.5g); Cholesterol 35mg; Sodium 100mg; Total Carbohydrate 26g (Dietary Fiber 0g); Protein 3g EXCHANGES: ½ Starch, 1½ Other Carbohydrate, 2 Fat CARBOHYDRATE CHOICES: 2

sweet note Look for the almond paste in the baking aisle of the grocery store. It should be fresh and fairly pliable, so check the freshness date on the package.

almond streusel–cherry cheesecake bars

prep time: **45 minutes**   *start to finish:* **4 hours**   [24 BARS]

cookie base and topping

1 pouch (1 lb 1.5 oz) Betty Crocker sugar cookie mix

¼ cup cold butter or margarine

4 oz (half of 8-oz package) cream cheese

½ cup sliced almonds

filling

2½ packages (8 oz each) cream cheese (20 oz), softened

½ cup sugar

2 tablespoons all-purpose flour

1 teaspoon almond extract

2 eggs

1 can (21 oz) cherry pie filling

1   Heat oven to 350°F. Spray bottom and sides of 13 × 9-inch pan with cooking spray.

2   Place cookie mix in large bowl. Cut in butter and 4 oz cream cheese, using pastry blender or fork, until mixture is crumbly. Reserve 1½ cups mixture for topping. Set almonds aside. Press remaining crumb mixture in bottom of pan.

3   Bake 12 minutes. Meanwhile, in large bowl, beat 20 oz cream cheese, the sugar, flour, almond extract and eggs with electric mixer on medium speed until smooth.

4   Spread cream cheese mixture evenly over partially baked cookie base. Spoon pie filling evenly over cream cheese layer. Sprinkle with reserved topping and almonds.

5   Bake 40 to 45 minutes longer or until light golden brown. Cool 30 minutes. Refrigerate about 2 hours or until chilled.

6   For bars, cut into 6 rows by 4 rows. Store covered in refrigerator.

1 BAR: Calories 270; Total Fat 15g (Saturated Fat 8g; Trans Fat 1g); Cholesterol 55mg; Sodium 160mg; Total Carbohydrate 28g (Dietary Fiber 0g); Protein 4g EXCHANGES: 1 Starch, 1 Other Carbohydrate, 3 Fat CARBOHYDRATE CHOICES: 2

sweet note Cheesecake in an easy bar—yum! You'll need a total of three 8-ounce packages of cream cheese for this recipe.

chocolate chip truffle bars

prep time: **35 minutes**   *start to finish:* **2 hours**   [35 BARS]

½ cup butter or margarine, softened

1 egg

1 pouch (1 lb 1.5 oz) Betty Crocker chocolate chip cookie mix

1 cup semisweet chocolate chips (6 oz)

1 container (1 lb) chocolate creamy ready-to-spread frosting

1 can (6.4 oz) pink decorating icing

35 yogurt-covered miniature pretzels

1 Heat oven to 350°F. Spray bottom only of 13 × 9-inch pan with cooking spray.

2 In medium bowl, stir together butter and egg. Stir in cookie mix until soft dough forms. Press mixture in bottom of pan using floured fingers.

3 Bake 19 to 21 minutes or until golden brown. Cool 30 minutes.

4 In medium microwavable bowl, microwave chocolate chips uncovered on High 1 to 2 minutes, stirring every 30 seconds, until melted. Stir in frosting. Spread evenly over bars. Cool completely, about 30 minutes.

5 For bars, cut into 7 rows by 5 rows. Using star tip on pink decorating icing, fill in each hole of each pretzel, forming a heart in center. Place decorated pretzel on each bar.

1 BAR: Calories 190; Total Fat 10g (Saturated Fat 5g; Trans Fat 0g); Cholesterol 15mg; Sodium 150mg; Total Carbohydrate 25g (Dietary Fiber 0g); Protein 1g EXCHANGES: ½ Starch, 1 Other Carbohydrate, 2 Fat CARBOHYDRATE CHOICES: 1½

sweet note For easy removal, line your pan with foil, then spray the foil with the cooking spray. When the bars are cooled, you can easily lift them from the pan for cutting.

fiesta fudge cookies

prep time: 1 hour   *start to finish:* 1 hour   [5 DOZEN COOKIES]

⅓ cup butter or margarine

6 oz unsweetened baking chocolate

1 can (14 oz) sweetened condensed milk (not evaporated)

1 pouch (1 lb 1.5 oz) Betty Crocker sugar cookie mix

1 teaspoon ground cinnamon

60 white and chocolate–striped candy drops or pieces, unwrapped

1 Heat oven to 350°F.

2 In large microwavable bowl, microwave butter and chocolate on High 1 minute. Stir; microwave on High 1 minute longer or until butter is melted and chocolate can be stirred smooth. Stir condensed milk into chocolate mixture. Stir in cookie mix and cinnamon until well blended.

3 Using 1 level tablespoonful of dough for each cookie, shape into 60 balls. On ungreased cookie sheets, place balls about 2 inches apart.

4 Bake 6 to 9 minutes or until edges lose their shiny look (do not overbake). Immediately press 1 candy into center of each cookie. Cool cookies on cookie sheet 5 minutes; remove from cookie sheets. To get candy to spread slightly on top of cookie, tap edge of each cookie lightly. Cool completely. Store covered at room temperature.

1 COOKIE: Calories 110; Total Fat 5g (Saturated Fat 2.5g; Trans Fat 0g); Cholesterol 5mg; Sodium 40mg; Total Carbohydrate 14g (Dietary Fiber 0g); Protein 2g EXCHANGES: ½ Starch, ½ Other Carbohydrate, 1 Fat CARBOHYDRATE CHOICES: 1

sweet note Milk chocolate candy drops can be substituted for the striped candy.

easy monster cookies

prep time: 1 hour *start to finish:* 1 hour [1½ DOZEN COOKIES]

1 pouch (1 lb 1.5 oz) Betty Crocker chocolate chip cookie mix

1 pouch (1 lb 1.5 oz) Betty Crocker peanut butter cookie mix

1½ cups quick-cooking oats

1 cup butter or margarine, softened

3 eggs

2 cups candy-coated milk chocolate candies

1 Heat oven to 375°F.

2 In large bowl, stir all ingredients except candies until soft dough forms. Stir in candies. On ungreased cookie sheets, place about ¼ cupfuls dough about 3 inches apart.

3 Bake 12 to 13 minutes or until light golden brown. Cool 2 minutes; remove from cookie sheets to cooling racks. Store cooled cookies in covered container at room temperature.

1 COOKIE: Calories 480; Total Fat 23g (Saturated Fat 12g; Trans Fat 0g); Cholesterol 65mg; Sodium 340mg; Total Carbohydrate 61g (Dietary Fiber 1g); Protein 6g EXCHANGES: 2 Starch, 2 Other Carbohydrate, 4½ Fat CARBOHYDRATE CHOICES: 4

sweet note To make 3 dozen smaller cookies, for each cookie, drop dough by 2 heaping tablespoonfuls about 2 inches apart on ungreased cookie sheets. Bake 10 to 12 minutes.

nanaimo cookie bars

prep time: **45 minutes**   *start to finish:* **2 hours 5 minutes**   [36 BARS]

cookie base

1 pouch (1 lb 1.5 oz) Betty Crocker double chocolate chunk cookie mix

1 cup graham cracker crumbs

½ cup chopped nut topping or chopped walnuts

½ cup flaked coconut

1 cup butter or margarine, melted

1 egg

filling

4 cups powdered sugar

4 tablespoons vanilla instant pudding and pie filling mix

⅓ cup butter or margarine, softened

¼ cup milk

topping

1 bag (12 oz) semisweet chocolate chips (2 cups)

¼ cup butter or margarine

1 Heat oven to 350°F. Line bottom and sides of 13 × 9-inch pan with foil, leaving foil overhanging at 2 opposite sides of pan.

2 In large bowl, stir cookie base ingredients until well mixed. Spread into pan; press lightly.

3 Bake 16 to 18 minutes or until set. Cool completely, about 30 minutes.

4 In another large bowl, stir together powdered sugar and dry pudding mix. Add ⅓ cup butter and the milk; beat with electric mixer on medium speed until smooth (filling will be very thick). Spoon over cookie base; press evenly to cover. Refrigerate while making topping.

5 In small microwavable bowl, microwave topping ingredients uncovered on High 1 minute to 1 minute 30 seconds, stirring every 30 seconds until melted and smooth. Spread over filling. Refrigerate uncovered until set, about 30 minutes.

6 Use foil to lift bars from pan; pull foil from sides of bars. Cut into 9 rows by 4 rows. Store covered in refrigerator.

1 BAR: Calories 270; Total Fat 14g (Saturated Fat 8g; Trans Fat 0g); Cholesterol 25mg; Sodium 150mg; Total Carbohydrate 34g (Dietary Fiber 0g); Protein 1g EXCHANGES: ½ Starch, 1½ Other Carbohydrate, 3 Fat CARBOHYDRATE CHOICES: 2

sweet note Canadian legend claims that these yummy bars originated in Nanaimo, Canada, in the 1950s. Although unsubstantiated, the story is that a local housewife submitted the recipe under the name "Nanaimo Bars" for a recipe contest.

candy-topped blossom cookies

prep time: **1 hour 35 minutes** *start to finish:* **2 hours 5 minutes** [4 DOZEN COOKIES]

1 can (14 oz) sweetened condensed milk (not evaporated)

1 cup creamy peanut butter

2 cups Original Bisquick mix

1 teaspoon vanilla

3 tablespoons sugar

48 round chewy caramels in milk chocolate (from 12-oz bag), unwrapped

1 Heat oven to 375°F.

2 In large bowl, beat condensed milk and peanut butter with electric mixer on medium speed until well blended. Stir in Bisquick mix and vanilla until well blended.

3 Shape dough into 48 (1-inch) balls. Measure sugar into small bowl. Dip top of each ball into sugar. On ungreased cookie sheets, place balls 2 inches apart.

4 Bake 7 to 9 minutes. Firmly press 1 caramel into center of each cookie. Bake about 1 minute longer or until chocolate begins to soften and cookie begins to turn light golden brown. Cool 2 to 3 minutes; remove from cookie sheets to cooling racks. Cool completely, about 30 minutes.

1 COOKIE: Calories 110; Total Fat 5g (Saturated Fat 2g; Trans Fat 0g); Cholesterol 0mg; Sodium 110mg; Total Carbohydrate 14g (Dietary Fiber 0g); Protein 2g EXCHANGES: ½ Starch, ½ Other Carbohydrate, 1 Fat CARBOHYDRATE CHOICES: 1

sweet note If you like, chunky peanut butter can be used instead of the creamy type. The cookies will have a crunchier texture.

ultimate turtle brownies

prep time: **30 minutes**   *start to finish:* **3 hours 5 minutes**   [24 BROWNIES]

1 box (1 lb 2.4 oz) Betty Crocker Original Supreme Premium brownie mix

Water, vegetable oil and egg called for on brownie mix box

36 caramels (from 14-oz bag), unwrapped

3 tablespoons whipping cream

1⅓ cups semisweet chocolate chunks

⅔ cup coarsely chopped pecans

1   Heat oven to 350°F (325°F for dark or nonstick pan). Spray bottom and sides of 9-inch square pan with baking spray with flour.

2   Make brownie mix as directed on box, using pouch of chocolate syrup, water, oil and egg. Spread ½ of batter in pan. Bake 18 minutes.

3   Meanwhile, in large microwavable bowl, microwave caramels and whipping cream uncovered on High 2 to 3 minutes, stirring occasionally, until smooth.

4   Pour caramel mixture over partially baked brownie; spread to within ¼ inch of edges. Sprinkle with ⅔ cup of the chocolate chunks and ⅓ cup of the pecans. Drop remaining brownie batter by small spoonfuls onto caramel layer. Sprinkle with remaining ⅔ cup chocolate chunks and ⅓ cup pecans.

5   Bake 34 to 37 minutes longer or until center is almost set. Cool 1 hour at room temperature. Cover; refrigerate 1 hour before serving.

6   For brownies, cut into 6 rows by 4 rows. Store covered at room temperature.

1 BROWNIE: Calories 250; Total Fat 11g (Saturated Fat 3g; Trans Fat 0g); Cholesterol 20mg; Sodium 115mg; Total Carbohydrate 36g (Dietary Fiber 1g); Protein 2g EXCHANGES: ½ Starch, 2 Other Carbohydrate, 2 Fat CARBOHYDRATE CHOICES: 2½

sweet note You'll get rave reviews when you tote these caramelicious brownies to your next bake sale or potluck. You can make them the day ahead and store tightly covered at room temperature so they are ready to go when you are!

peanut butter truffle brownies

prep time: **20 minutes**   *start to finish:* **2 hours 30 minutes**   [36 BROWNIES]

brownie base

1 box (1 lb 2.3 oz) Betty Crocker fudge brownie mix

Water, vegetable oil and eggs called for on brownie mix box

filling

½ cup butter or margarine, softened

½ cup creamy peanut butter

2 cups powdered sugar

2 teaspoons milk

topping

1 cup semisweet chocolate chips

¼ cup butter or margarine, softened

1 Heat oven to 350°F. Grease bottom only of 13 × 9-inch pan with shortening or cooking spray. (For easier cutting, line pan with foil, then grease foil on bottom only of pan.)

2 Make brownies as directed on box using water, oil and eggs. Bake as directed on box for 13 × 9-inch pan. Cool completely, about 1 hour.

3 In medium bowl, beat filling ingredients with electric mixer on medium speed until smooth. Spread mixture evenly over brownie base.

4 In small microwavable bowl, microwave topping ingredients uncovered on High 30 to 60 seconds; stir until smooth. Cool 10 minutes; spread over filling. Refrigerate about 30 minutes or until set.

5 For brownies, cut into 9 rows by 4 rows. Store covered in refrigerator.

1 BROWNIE: Calories 200; Total Fat 12g (Saturated Fat 4.5g; Trans Fat 0g); Cholesterol 20mg; Sodium 100mg; Total Carbohydrate 23g (Dietary Fiber 0g); Protein 1g EXCHANGES: 1½ Other Carbohydrate, 2½ Fat CARBOHYDRATE CHOICES: 1½

sweet note These brownies are ideal for a dessert buffet. Cut them into bite-size squares and arrange on a decorative platter for serving.

mexican brownies

prep time: 30 minutes   *start to finish:* 3 hours   [16 BROWNIES]

1 box (1 lb 2.4 oz) Betty Crocker Original Supreme Premium brownie mix

2 teaspoons ground cinnamon

Water, vegetable oil and egg called for on brownie mix box

⅔ cup semisweet chocolate chips

⅓ cup butter or margarine

⅔ cup packed brown sugar

3 tablespoons milk

1½ cups powdered sugar

⅔ cup chopped pecans, toasted*

1 Heat oven to 350°F (325°F for dark or nonstick pan). Spray bottom only of 8- or 9-inch square pan with cooking spray.

2 In medium bowl, stir together dry brownie mix and cinnamon. Add pouch of chocolate syrup, water, oil and egg; stir until well blended. Stir in chocolate chips. Spread in pan.

3 Bake as directed on brownie mix box for 8- or 9-inch square pan. Cool completely, about 2 hours.

4 In 2-quart saucepan, melt butter over medium heat. Stir in brown sugar. Heat to boiling, stirring constantly. Reduce heat to low; boil and stir 2 minutes. Stir in milk. Heat to boiling. Remove from heat; cool to lukewarm, about 30 minutes.

5 Gradually beat powdered sugar into brown sugar mixture with whisk until blended, then beat until smooth. If frosting becomes too stiff, stir in additional milk, 1 teaspoon at a time. Spread frosting over brownies; sprinkle with pecans.

6 For brownies, cut into 4 rows by 4 rows. Store tightly covered.

sweet note Lots of cinnamon, caramel and pecans provide the Mexican flair in these decadent brownies.

To toast pecans, bake in ungreased shallow pan in 350°F oven about 10 minutes, stirring occasionally, until golden brown.

1 BROWNIE: Calories 360; Total Fat 16g (Saturated Fat 5g; Trans Fat 0g); Cholesterol 35mg; Sodium 140mg; Total Carbohydrate 53g (Dietary Fiber 1g); Protein 2g EXCHANGES: ½ Starch, 3 Other Carbohydrate, 3 Fat CARBOHYDRATE CHOICES: 3½

brownie goody bars

prep time: **15 minutes**   *start to finish:* **3 hours 55 minutes**   [24 BARS]

1 box (1 lb 2.3 oz) Betty Crocker fudge brownie mix

Water, vegetable oil and eggs called for on brownie mix box

1 container (12 oz to 1 lb) vanilla whipped or vanilla creamy ready-to-spread frosting

¾ cup salted peanuts, coarsely chopped

3 cups crisp rice cereal

1 cup creamy peanut butter

1 bag (12 oz) semisweet chocolate chips (2 cups)

1   Heat oven to 350°F. Spray bottom only of 13 × 9-inch pan with cooking spray.

2   Make brownie mix as directed on box, using water, oil and eggs. Spread batter into pan.

3   Bake as directed on box for 13 × 9-inch pan. Cool completely, about 1 hour.

4   Spread brownies with frosting; sprinkle with peanuts. Refrigerate while making cereal mixture.

5   Into large bowl, measure cereal; set aside. In 1-quart saucepan, melt peanut butter and chocolate chips over low heat, stirring constantly. Pour over cereal in bowl, stirring until evenly coated. Spread over frosted brownies. Cool completely before cutting, about 1 hour.

6   For bars, cut into 6 rows by 4 rows. Store tightly covered at room temperature or in refrigerator.

1 BAR: Calories 370; Total Fat 18g (Saturated Fat 5g; Trans Fat 1g); Cholesterol 10mg; Sodium 160mg; Total Carbohydrate 45g (Dietary Fiber 2g); Protein 4g EXCHANGES: 1 Starch, 2 Other Carbohydrate, 3½ Fat CARBOHYDRATE CHOICES: 3

sweet note These are incredibly rich bars that can be served with a fork. For even more decadence, top off each serving with a drizzle of caramel topping.

peanutty granola cookies

prep time: 1 hour   *start to finish:* 1 hour 45 minutes   [32 COOKIES]

1 box (1 lb 2.25 oz) Betty Crocker SuperMoist butter recipe yellow cake mix

½ cup butter or margarine, softened

2 eggs

4 peanut granola bars (from 7.4-oz box), coarsely chopped

½ cup peanut butter chips (from 10-oz bag)

1½ teaspoons shortening

1 Heat oven to 350°F (325°F for dark or nonstick pan).

2 In large bowl, beat cake mix, butter and eggs with electric mixer on medium speed until smooth. Stir in granola bars. Onto ungreased cookie sheet, drop dough by tablespoonfuls 2 inches apart.

3 Bake 10 to 12 minutes or until set and light golden brown around edges. Cool 2 minutes; remove from cookie sheet to cooling rack. Cool completely, about 30 minutes.

4 In microwavable food-storage plastic bag, place peanut butter chips and shortening; seal bag. Microwave on High 15 seconds; squeeze bag. Microwave 15 to 25 seconds longer or until melted; squeeze bag until mixture is smooth. Cut off tiny corner of bag; squeeze bag to drizzle mixture over cookies. Let stand about 10 minutes or until drizzle is set. Store in airtight container.

1 COOKIE: Calories 120; Total Fat 6g (Saturated Fat 2.5g; Trans Fat 0g); Cholesterol 20mg; Sodium 150mg; Total Carbohydrate 16g (Dietary Fiber 0g); Protein 1g EXCHANGES: 1 Other Carbohydrate, 1½ Fat CARBOHYDRATE CHOICES: 1

sweet note Semisweet or dark chocolate chips would be a nice alternative to the peanut butter chips in this recipe.

fudge crinkles

prep time: 1 hour   *start to finish:* 1 hour   [2½ DOZEN COOKIES]

1 box (1 lb 2.25 oz) Betty Crocker SuperMoist devil's food cake mix

½ cup vegetable oil

2 eggs

1 teaspoon vanilla

⅓ cup powdered sugar

1   Heat oven to 350°F.

2   In large bowl, mix cake mix, oil, eggs and vanilla with spoon until dough forms.

3   Shape dough into 30 (1-inch) balls. Roll balls in powdered sugar. On ungreased cookie sheet, place balls about 2 inches apart.

4   Bake 10 to 12 minutes or until set. Cool 1 minute; remove from cookie sheet to cooling rack. Store cooled cookies tightly covered.

1 COOKIE: Calories 110; Total Fat 5g (Saturated Fat 1g; Trans Fat 0g); Cholesterol 15mg; Sodium 140mg; Total Carbohydrate 15g (Dietary Fiber 0g); Protein 1g EXCHANGES: 1 Other Carbohydrate, 1 Fat CARBOHYDRATE CHOICES: 1

sweet note For an extra flavor treat, stir 1 cup miniature candy-coated chocolate baking bits into the dough. Or, instead of rolling the cookies in powdered sugar, dip the tops into chocolate candy sprinkles before baking.

cookie gifts

Cookies and bars are perfect for sending to loved ones. Here are some tips to make sure they arrive at the destination intact.

- **Wrap cookies in pairs,** back to back.
- **Brownies and bars will remain fresher** if left uncut— just wrap the whole rectangle in foil to be cut later.
- **Use rigid plastic containers,** metal tins or firm-sided cardboard boxes for packing.
- **Fill each container** until almost full and use crumpled waxed paper or paper towels for cushioning.
- **Pack filled containers** in a firm cardboard box. Cushion with bubble wrap, crumpled paper or packing peanuts.

carrot-spice cookies

prep time: 1 hour   *start to finish:* 1 hour 25 minutes   [ABOUT 4 DOZEN COOKIES]

cookies

1 box (1 lb 2 oz) Betty Crocker SuperMoist carrot cake mix

¼ cup all-purpose flour

½ cup butter or margarine, melted

2 eggs

1 cup sweetened dried cranberries

glaze

½ cup cream cheese creamy ready-to-spread frosting (from 1-lb container)

1 Heat oven to 350°F.

2 In large bowl, beat cake mix, flour, butter and eggs with electric mixer on low speed 1 minute. Stir in cranberries. Onto ungreased cookie sheets, drop dough by teaspoonfuls about 2 inches apart.

3 Bake 10 to 12 minutes or until edges are set. Immediately remove from cookie sheets to cooling racks. Cool completely, about 10 minutes.

4 In small microwavable bowl, microwave frosting on High 10 to 15 seconds or until frosting is thin enough to drizzle. Drizzle frosting over cookies.

1 COOKIE: Calories 80; Total Fat 3g (Saturated Fat 1.5g; Trans Fat 0g); Cholesterol 15mg; Sodium 85mg; Total Carbohydrate 12g (Dietary Fiber 0g); Protein 0g EXCHANGES: 1 Other Carbohydrate, ½ Fat CARBOHYDRATE CHOICES: 1

sweet note Regular raisins, golden raisins or dried cherries could be substituted for the cranberries in these tasty cookies.

glazed lemon wedges

prep time: **15 minutes**   *start to finish:* **1 hour 40 minutes**   [24 COOKIE WEDGES]

cookies

1 box (1 lb 2.25 oz) Betty Crocker SuperMoist butter recipe yellow cake mix

½ cup butter or margarine, softened

2 tablespoons grated lemon peel

1 egg

glaze

1 cup powdered sugar

1 teaspoon grated lemon peel

3 tablespoons lemon juice

garnish

Grated lemon peel, if desired

1 Heat oven to 350°F (325°F for dark or nonstick pans). Spray bottoms and sides of 2 (8-inch) round cake pans with baking spray with flour or line with foil.

2 In large bowl, beat cake mix, butter, 2 tablespoons lemon peel and the egg with electric mixer on low speed until crumbly. Beat on medium speed until dough forms. Press half of dough in each pan.

3 Bake 18 to 22 minutes or until edges are light golden brown. Cool 10 minutes.

4 In small bowl, mix glaze ingredients until smooth. Spoon glaze over warm shortbread; spread to edges of pans. Cool completely, about 50 minutes. Garnish with lemon peel. Cut each shortbread into 12 wedges.

1 COOKIE WEDGE: Calories 140; Total Fat 6g (Saturated Fat 3g; Trans Fat 0.5g); Cholesterol 20mg; Sodium 170mg; Total Carbohydrate 22g (Dietary Fiber 0g); Protein 1g EXCHANGES: ½ Starch, 1 Other Carbohydrate, 1 Fat CARBOHYDRATE CHOICES: 1½

sweet note When grating the lemon peel, be sure to grate only the yellow part of the skin. The white part, or pith, is very bitter.

chunky chocolate and almond bars

prep time: 20 minutes   *start to finish:* 2 hours 35 minutes   [48 BARS]

base

1 box (1 lb 2.25 oz) Betty Crocker SuperMoist chocolate fudge cake mix

½ cup butter or margarine, softened

topping

4 eggs

1 cup dark corn syrup

¼ cup butter or margarine, melted

2 cups salted roasted whole almonds, coarsely chopped

6 oz dark or bittersweet baking chocolate, chopped

1 Heat oven to 350°F (325°F for dark or nonstick pan).

2 Place cake mix in medium bowl. Using pastry blender or fork, cut in softened butter until crumbly. Press firmly in ungreased 13 × 9-inch pan. Bake 12 to 14 minutes or until set.

3 In large bowl, beat eggs, corn syrup and melted butter with whisk until smooth. Stir in almonds and chocolate. Pour over base.

4 Bake 25 to 30 minutes longer or until golden brown and set. Cool 30 minutes. Refrigerate about 1 hour or until chocolate is firm.

5 For bars, cut into 8 rows by 6 rows. Store covered in refrigerator.

1 BAR: Calories 150; Total Fat 9g (Saturated Fat 3.5g; Trans Fat 0g); Cholesterol 25mg; Sodium 135mg; Total Carbohydrate 15g (Dietary Fiber 1g); Protein 2g EXCHANGES: 1 Starch, 1½ Fat CARBOHYDRATE CHOICES: 1

sweet note Much like the center of a pecan pie, the center of these bars is very moist and may even look raw. Not to worry—that's how they should look.

chapter five

fruit desserts

brownie 'n berries dessert pizza

prep time: **20 minutes**   *start to finish:* **2 hours 50 minutes**   [16 SERVINGS]

1 box (1 lb 2.3 oz) Betty Crocker fudge brownie mix

Water, vegetable oil and eggs called for on brownie mix box

1 package (8 oz) cream cheese, softened

⅓ cup sugar

½ teaspoon vanilla

2 cups sliced fresh strawberries

1 cup fresh blueberries

1 cup fresh raspberries

½ cup apple jelly

1 Heat oven to 350°F. Grease bottom only of 12-inch pizza pan with shortening or cooking spray.

2 In medium bowl, stir brownie mix, water, oil and eggs until well blended. Spread in pan.

3 Bake 24 to 26 minutes or until toothpick inserted 2 inches from side of pan comes out clean or almost clean. Cool completely, about 1 hour.

4 In small bowl, beat cream cheese, sugar and vanilla with electric mixer on medium speed until smooth. Spread mixture evenly over brownie base. Arrange berries over cream cheese mixture. Stir jelly until smooth; brush over berries. Refrigerate about 1 hour or until chilled.

5 Cut into wedges. Store covered in refrigerator.

1 SERVING: Calories 320; Total Fat 15g (Saturated Fat 4.5g; Trans Fat 0g); Cholesterol 40mg; Sodium 170mg; Total Carbohydrate 44g (Dietary Fiber 1g); Protein 2g EXCHANGES: ½ Starch, ½ Fruit, 2 Other Carbohydrate, 3 Fat CARBOHYDRATE CHOICES: 3

sweet note For easy cleanup, bake the brownie in a 12-inch disposable foil pizza pan. Slide the pan onto a cookie sheet when you remove the brownie from the oven. Place the brownie dessert on a tray when you take it to the table.

white chocolate–berry bread pudding

prep time: **30 minutes**   *start to finish:* **10 hours 10 minutes**   [12 SERVINGS]

pudding

4½ cups Original Bisquick mix

1⅓ cups milk

¾ cup grated white chocolate baking bars

⅔ cup sugar

3½ cups milk

1½ cups whipping cream

2 tablespoons butter or margarine, melted

1 tablespoon vanilla

4 eggs

1 cup frozen unsweetened raspberries (do not thaw)

1 cup frozen unsweetened blueberries (do not thaw)

berry sauce and garnish

⅓ cup sugar

2 tablespoons Original Bisquick mix

1 cup frozen unsweetened raspberries (do not thaw)

1 cup frozen unsweetened blueberries (do not thaw)

½ cup water

Fresh berries, if desired

1 Heat oven to 450°F. Butter bottom and sides of 13 × 9-inch (3-quart) glass baking dish.

2 In large bowl, stir 4½ cups Bisquick mix and 1⅓ cups milk until soft dough forms. Onto ungreased large cookie sheet, drop dough by heaping tablespoonfuls. Bake 8 to 10 minutes or until golden. Cool on cooling rack, about 30 minutes.

3 Break up biscuits into random-sized pieces; spread in baking dish. Sprinkle with grated baking bars. In large bowl, beat ⅔ cup sugar, 3½ cups milk, whipping cream, butter, vanilla and eggs with electric mixer on low speed until blended. Pour over biscuits in baking dish. Cover; refrigerate at least 8 hours but no longer than 24 hours.

4 Heat oven to 350°F. Stir 1 cup frozen raspberries and 1 cup frozen blueberries into biscuit mixture. Bake uncovered about 1 hour or until top is golden brown and toothpick inserted in center comes out clean.

5 In 1-quart saucepan, place ⅓ cup sugar and 2 tablespoons Bisquick mix. Stir in 1 cup frozen raspberries, 1 cup frozen blueberries and the water. Cook over medium heat, stirring constantly, until mixture thickens and boils. Boil and stir 1 minute; remove from heat. Serve pudding warm topped with sauce. Garnish with fresh berries. Store in refrigerator.

1 SERVING: Calories 530; Total Fat 24g (Saturated Fat 12g; Trans Fat 2g); Cholesterol 120mg; Sodium 660mg; Total Carbohydrate 67g (Dietary Fiber 5g); Protein 11g EXCHANGES: 3 Starch, 1½ Other Carbohydrate, 4½ Fat CARBOHYDRATE CHOICES: 4½

sweet note In this recipe, drop biscuits rather than rolled biscuits are made to give more of a crusty brown surface to the pudding.

southern apple crumble

prep time: **20 minutes**   *start to finish:* **1 hour 20 minutes**   [9 SERVINGS]

apple mixture

3 large apples, peeled, coarsely chopped (about 3 cups)

½ cup granulated sugar

¼ cup packed brown sugar

1 to 2 teaspoons ground cinnamon

¼ cup cold butter or margarine, cut into small pieces

topping

1 pouch (1 lb 1.5 oz) Betty Crocker oatmeal cookie mix

½ cup butter or margarine, melted

½ cup chopped pecans

sweet note If you've got juicy fresh peaches, you can substitute them for the apples and make a peach crumble instead. Top either version with whipped cream or ice cream.

1   Heat oven to 300°F. Spray bottom and sides of 8-inch square (2-quart) glass baking dish with cooking spray.

2   In large bowl, toss apple mixture ingredients. Spread mixture in baking dish. In same large bowl, stir cookie mix and melted butter until crumbly. Sprinkle over top of apple mixture.

3   Bake 40 minutes. Remove from oven; sprinkle with pecans. Bake 15 to 20 minutes longer or until topping is golden brown. Serve warm or at room temperature.

1 SERVING: Calories 480; Total Fat 22g (Saturated Fat 10g; Trans Fat 0.5g); Cholesterol 40mg; Sodium 320mg; Total Carbohydrate 67g (Dietary Fiber 2g); Protein 5g EXCHANGES: 1½ Starch, 3 Other Carbohydrate, 4 Fat CARBOHYDRATE CHOICES: 4½

fabulous fruit

For unsurpassed freshness and flavor, look for locally grown fruit for your dessert at grocery stores, farmers' markets or roadside stands. Consumer information is often paired with fruit displays, or ask the purveyor which varieties are best for baking, cooking and eating.

strawberries and cream dessert squares

prep time: **30 minutes**   *start to finish:* **2 hours 30 minutes**   [20 SERVINGS]

crust

1 pouch (1 lb 1.5 oz) Betty Crocker sugar cookie mix

½ cup butter or margarine, softened

1 egg

filling

1 cup white vanilla baking chips (6 oz)

1 package (8 oz) cream cheese, softened

topping

4 cups sliced fresh strawberries

½ cup sugar

2 tablespoons cornstarch

⅓ cup water

10 to 12 drops red food color, if desired

1   Heat oven to 350°F. Spray bottom only of 15 × 10 × 1- or 13 × 9-inch pan with cooking spray.

2   In large bowl, stir cookie mix, butter and egg until soft dough forms. Press evenly in bottom of pan.

3   Bake 15 to 20 minutes or until light golden brown. Cool completely, about 30 minutes.

4   In small microwavable bowl, microwave baking chips uncovered on High 45 to 60 seconds or until chips are melted and can be stirred smooth. In medium bowl, beat cream cheese with electric mixer on medium speed until smooth. Stir in melted chips until blended. Spread mixture over crust. Refrigerate while making topping.

5   In small bowl, crush 1 cup of the strawberries. In 2-quart saucepan, mix sugar and cornstarch. Stir in crushed strawberries and the water. Cook over medium heat, stirring constantly, until mixture boils and thickens. Stir in food color. Cool 10 minutes. Gently stir in remaining 3 cups strawberries. Spoon over filling. Refrigerate 1 hour or until set; serve within 4 hours.

1 SERVING: Calories 270; Total Fat 13g (Saturated Fat 8g; Trans Fat 1g); Cholesterol 35mg; Sodium 150mg; Total Carbohydrate 34g (Dietary Fiber 0g); Protein 3g EXCHANGES: 1 Starch, 1 Other Carbohydrate, 2½ Fat CARBOHYDRATE CHOICES: 2

sweet note Strawberries are available most times of the year. Look for those that are bright red with green caps still attached. They should look fresh and have no signs of mold or decay.

peach crisp

prep time: **10 minutes**   *start to finish:* **40 minutes**   [6 SERVINGS]

1 pouch (1 lb 1.5 oz) Betty Crocker oatmeal cookie mix

½ cup cold butter

5 cups frozen sliced peaches, thawed, drained, or 1 can (29 oz) sliced peaches, drained

1 Heat oven to 375°F.

2 In large bowl, place cookie mix. Cut in butter, using pastry blender or fork, until mixture looks like coarse crumbs.

3 In ungreased 8-inch square (2-quart) glass baking dish, place peaches. Sprinkle cookie mixture over peaches.

4 Bake 25 to 30 minutes or until topping is golden brown. Serve warm or cool.

1 SERVING: Calories 650; Total Fat 19g (Saturated Fat 10g; Trans Fat 0.5g); Cholesterol 40mg; Sodium 440mg; Total Carbohydrate 113g (Dietary Fiber 5g); Protein 7g EXCHANGES: 2 Starch, 1 Fruit, 4½ Other Carbohydrate, 3½ Fat CARBOHYDRATE CHOICES: 7½

sweet note Top this yummy dessert with vanilla or cinnamon ice cream, or sweetened whipped cream.

cinnamon-peach cobbler

prep time: **15** minutes   *start to finish:* **40** minutes   [12 SERVINGS]

peach mixture

¼ cup butter or margarine

½ cup sugar

2 tablespoons cornstarch

2 teaspoons ground
cinnamon

½ teaspoon ground nutmeg

2 teaspoons vanilla

½ teaspoon lemon extract

2 jars (24.5 oz each) sliced
peaches in light syrup,
drained, 1½ cups syrup
reserved

topping

2 cups Bisquick Heart
Smart® mix

3 tablespoons sugar

¼ teaspoon ground
cinnamon

½ cup milk

1 tablespoon butter or
margarine, melted

1 Heat oven to 400°F.

2 In 4-quart saucepan, heat ¼ cup butter, ½ cup sugar and the cornstarch over medium heat 1 minute, stirring constantly, until butter
is melted. Stir in 2 teaspoons cinnamon, the nutmeg, vanilla, lemon
extract and peaches with reserved syrup. Heat to boiling; boil
1 minute, stirring occasionally. Pour into ungreased 13 × 9-inch
(3-quart) glass baking dish.

3 In medium bowl, stir Bisquick mix, 2 tablespoons of the sugar,
¼ teaspoon cinnamon, the milk and melted butter until soft dough
forms. Drop dough by heaping tablespoonfuls onto hot peach
mixture. Sprinkle with remaining 1 tablespoon sugar.

4 Bake 20 to 25 minutes or until peach mixture is bubbly around edges
and topping is golden brown. Serve warm.

1 SERVING: Calories 250; Total Fat 6g (Saturated Fat 3g; Trans Fat 0g); Cholesterol 15mg;
Sodium 210mg; Total Carbohydrate 44g (Dietary Fiber 2g); Protein 2g EXCHANGES: ½ Starch,
1 Fruit, 1½ Other Carbohydrate, 1 Fat CARBOHYDRATE CHOICES: 3

sweet note Add a little extra decadence by topping
servings of this dessert with frozen yogurt.

impossibly easy french apple dessert squares

prep time: 25 minutes   *start to finish:* 1 hour 50 minutes   [15 SERVINGS]

streusel

1 cup Original Bisquick mix

½ cup packed brown sugar

¼ cup cold butter or margarine

¾ cup chopped nuts

fruit mixture

6 cups sliced peeled tart apples (6 medium)

2 teaspoons ground cinnamon

½ teaspoon ground nutmeg

1 cup Original Bisquick mix

1 cup granulated sugar

1 cup milk

2 tablespoons butter or margarine, melted

4 eggs, beaten

1 Heat oven to 350°F. Spray 13 × 9-inch pan with cooking spray.

2 In medium bowl, mix 1 cup Bisquick mix and the brown sugar. Cut in ¼ cup butter, using pastry blender or fork, until crumbly. Stir in nuts; set aside.

3 In large bowl, mix apples, cinnamon and nutmeg; spoon into pan. In medium bowl, stir remaining ingredients until well blended. Pour mixture over apples. Sprinkle with streusel.

4 Bake 45 to 55 minutes or until knife inserted in center comes out clean and top is golden brown. Cool 30 minutes or until set before cutting into squares. Store in refrigerator.

1 SERVING: Calories 290; Total Fat 12g (Saturated Fat 5g; Trans Fat 1g); Cholesterol 70mg; Sodium 280mg; Total Carbohydrate 39g (Dietary Fiber 2g); Protein 4g EXCHANGES: 1 Starch, 1½ Other Carbohydrate, 2½ Fat CARBOHYDRATE CHOICES: 2½

sweet note Apple varieties that would be good for this recipe include Cortland, Rome Beauty, McIntosh, Granny Smith and Jonathon.

blueberry-peach cobbler with walnut biscuits

prep time: **30 minutes**   *start to finish:* **1 hour 40 minutes**   [6 SERVINGS]

fruit mixture

8 medium fresh peaches (about 2 lb), peeled, each cut into 6 wedges

1 cup fresh blueberries

1 tablespoon cornstarch

½ cup granulated sugar

1 tablespoon lemon juice

¼ teaspoon ground cinnamon

Dash salt

biscuit topping

1 cup Original Bisquick mix

¼ teaspoon ground nutmeg

2 tablespoons milk

2 tablespoons butter or margarine, softened

2 tablespoons granulated sugar

⅔ cup chopped walnuts

2 teaspoons milk, if desired

1 tablespoon coarse sugar

1 Heat oven to 400°F.

2 In medium bowl, stir together fruit mixture ingredients; let stand 10 minutes to allow sugar to pull juices from peaches. Transfer to ungreased 8-inch square (2-quart) glass baking dish.

3 Bake uncovered about 10 minutes or until fruit is bubbling. Remove from oven; stir. Bake 10 to 12 minutes longer or until bubbly around edges (fruit must be hot in middle so biscuit topping bakes completely).

4 Meanwhile, in medium bowl, stir all biscuit topping ingredients except 2 teaspoons milk and coarse sugar until firm dough forms. Drop dough by 6 spoonfuls onto warm fruit mixture. Brush dough with 2 teaspoons milk. Sprinkle with coarse sugar.

5 Bake 25 to 30 minutes or until biscuits are deep golden brown and center biscuit is no longer doughy on bottom. Cool 10 minutes on cooling rack. Serve warm.

1 SERVING: Calories 380; Total Fat 15g (Saturated Fat 4g; Trans Fat 1g); Cholesterol 10mg; Sodium 300mg; Total Carbohydrate 55g (Dietary Fiber 4g); Protein 5g EXCHANGES: 1½ Starch, 1 Fruit, 1 Other Carbohydrate, 3 Fat CARBOHYDRATE CHOICES: 3½

sweet note If fresh fruit is unavailable, it's easy to substitute frozen fruit. Use 1 cup frozen blueberries and 2 bags (16 ounces each) frozen sliced peaches instead. Thaw the frozen fruit before using.

creamy fruit tarts

prep time: 30 minutes   *start to finish:* 1 hour 15 minutes   [6 TARTS]

1 cup Original Bisquick mix

2 tablespoons sugar

1 tablespoon butter or margarine, softened

2 packages (3 oz each) cream cheese, softened

¼ cup sugar

¼ cup sour cream

1½ cups assorted sliced fresh fruit or berries

⅓ cup apple jelly, melted

1 Heat oven to 375°F.

2 In medium bowl, stir Bisquick mix, 2 tablespoons sugar, the butter and 1 package cream cheese in small bowl until dough forms a ball.

3 Divide dough into 6 parts. Press each part dough on bottom and ¾ inch up side in each of six 4-inch tart pans or 10-oz custard cups. Place on cookie sheet.

4 Bake 10 to 12 minutes or until light brown. Cool in pans on cooling rack, about 30 minutes. Remove tart shells from pans.

5 In small bowl, beat remaining package cream cheese, ¼ cup sugar and the sour cream until smooth. Spoon into tart shells, spreading over bottoms. Top each tart with about ¼ cup fruit. Brush with jelly.

1 TART: Calories 330; Total Fat 17g (Saturated Fat 9g; Trans Fat 1g); Cholesterol 45mg; Sodium 350mg; Total Carbohydrate 41g (Dietary Fiber 1g); Protein 4g EXCHANGES: 1 Starch, 1½ Other Carbohydrate, 3½ Fat CARBOHYDRATE CHOICES: 3

sweet note Use your imagination when choosing fruit for these tarts. Try sliced strawberries, kiwifruit, peaches or nectarines. Whole fruits such as raspberries, blueberries or blackberries are nice too.

chocolate chip–cherry cobbler

prep time: **15 minutes**   *start to finish:* **50 minutes**   [6 SERVINGS]

1 can (21 oz) cherry pie filling

2 tablespoons orange juice

½ teaspoon almond extract

1½ cups Original Bisquick mix

½ cup whipping cream

1 tablespoon sugar

1 tablespoon butter or margarine, softened

¼ cup miniature semisweet chocolate chips

½ teaspoon sugar

Chocolate syrup, if desired

1 Heat oven to 350°F.

2 In 1½-quart microwavable casserole, mix pie filling, orange juice and almond extract. Microwave uncovered on High about 4 minutes or until bubbly around edge; stir.

3 In medium bowl, mix remaining ingredients except ½ teaspoon sugar with spoon until stiff dough forms. Drop dough by 6 spoonfuls (about ¼ cup each) onto warm pie filling. Sprinkle ½ teaspoon sugar over dough.

4 Bake 30 to 35 minutes or until topping is golden brown. Serve warm, drizzled with chocolate syrup.

1 SERVING: Calories 350; Total Fat 15g (Saturated Fat 7g; Trans Fat 1g); Cholesterol 25mg; Sodium 450mg; Total Carbohydrate 50g (Dietary Fiber 2g); Protein 4g EXCHANGES: 1 Starch, 2½ Other Carbohydrate, 3 Fat CARBOHYDRATE CHOICES: 3

sweet note For a little more sparkle on top, sprinkle with 1 tablespoon coarse white sparkling sugar instead of the 1 teaspoon regular granulated sugar.

max quality

Usually, crisps, cobblers and some other fruit desserts are best the same day they're baked. The fruit often tends to soften the crisp topping. If you do have some dessert left over, reheat slightly before serving.

chocolate-strawberry shortcakes

prep time: 15 minutes   *start to finish:* 1 hour 45 minutes   [6 SHORTCAKES]

1 quart (4 cups) fresh
strawberries, sliced

½ cup sugar

2 cups Original Bisquick
mix

⅓ cup unsweetened
baking cocoa

2 tablespoons sugar

⅔ cup milk

2 tablespoons butter or
margarine, melted

⅓ cup miniature semisweet
chocolate chips

1½ cups frozen (thawed)
whipped topping

1 In medium bowl, toss strawberries and ½ cup sugar until coated.
Let stand 1 hour.

2 Heat oven to 375°F. Spray cookie sheet with cooking spray.

3 In medium bowl, stir Bisquick mix, cocoa, 2 tablespoons sugar,
the milk and butter until soft dough forms. Stir in chocolate chips.
Drop dough by about ⅓ cupfuls onto cookie sheet.

4 Bake 12 to 15 minutes or until tops of shortcakes appear dry and
cracked. Cool 15 minutes. Using serrated knife, split warm shortcakes. Fill with strawberries and whipped topping.

1 SHORTCAKE: Calories 460; Total Fat 17g (Saturated Fat 10g; Trans Fat 1.5g); Cholesterol 15mg;
Sodium 540mg; Total Carbohydrate 69g (Dietary Fiber 5g); Protein 6g EXCHANGES: 2 Starch,
1 Fruit, 1½ Other Carbohydrate, 3 Fat CARBOHYDRATE CHOICES: 4½

sweet note For the chocolate lovers in the family, sprinkle
additional miniature chocolate chips over tops of the shortcakes
before serving.

fresh fruit tart

prep time: 25 minutes   *start to finish:* 1 hour 15 minutes   [12 SERVINGS]

1 box (1 lb 2.25 oz) Betty Crocker SuperMoist lemon cake mix

½ cup butter or margarine, softened

1 egg

3 containers (6 oz each) fat-free lemon or French vanilla yogurt

1 box (4-serving size) vanilla instant pudding and pie filling mix

3 cups sliced fruits, berries and/or mandarin orange segments

3 tablespoons apricot preserves

1 cup fresh raspberries

1 Heat oven to 375°F (350°F for dark or nonstick pan). Grease 12-inch pizza pan or bottom only of 13 × 9-inch pan with shortening or cooking spray.

2 In large bowl, mix cake mix, butter and egg with spoon until crumbly. Press in bottom of pan.

3 Bake 14 to 18 minutes or until set. Cool completely, about 30 minutes.

4 In medium bowl, beat yogurt and pudding mix (dry) with electric mixer on medium speed until blended. Spoon over baked layer. Smooth surface with rubber spatula. Arrange fruit on yogurt mixture.

5 Heat preserves over medium heat until melted; brush over fruit. Mound raspberries in center. Serve immediately, or refrigerate up to 24 hours. Store covered in refrigerator.

1 SERVING: Calories 360; Total Fat 12g (Saturated Fat 6g; Trans Fat 1.5g); Cholesterol 40mg; Sodium 490mg; Total Carbohydrate 57g (Dietary Fiber 1g); Protein 4g EXCHANGES: 1 Starch, ½ Fruit, 2½ Other Carbohydrate, 2 Fat CARBOHYDRATE CHOICES: 4

sweet note In a hurry? A 21-ounce can of blueberry, cherry or apple pie filling can be substituted for the fruit, preserves and raspberries. Spoon the pie filling to within 1 inch of the edge of the yogurt mixture.

chapter six

other desserts

midnight molten brownie cupcakes

prep time: **10 minutes** *start to finish:* **30 minutes** [12 CUPCAKES]

½ cup semisweet chocolate chips

½ cup butter or margarine

3 eggs

3 egg yolks

1 box (1 lb 2.4 oz) Betty Crocker Original Supreme Premium brownie mix

About ½ cup stars, confetti or critters decors

1 Heat oven to 400°F. Generously grease 12 regular-size muffin cups with shortening or cooking spray.

2 In medium microwavable bowl, microwave chocolate chips and butter uncovered on High 45 to 60 seconds or until melted and mixture can be stirred smooth. Set aside.

3 In large bowl, beat eggs and egg yolks with whisk or electric mixer until foamy. Reserve chocolate syrup pouch from brownie mix. Gradually beat dry brownie mix into egg mixture until well blended. Gently stir in melted chocolate mixture. Fill muffin cups half full of brownie batter; top each with ½ teaspoon decors. Top with remaining brownie batter.

4 Bake 10 to 12 minutes or until edges are set. DO NOT OVERBAKE. Centers will be soft. Cool 2 minutes.

5 Loosen each cupcake with knife; turn upside down onto heatproof tray or cookie sheet. To serve, place cupcake on plate; drizzle with reserved chocolate syrup and top with additional decors.

1 CUPCAKE: Calories 300; Total Fat 14g (Saturated Fat 7g; Trans Fat 0g); Cholesterol 125mg; Sodium 220mg; Total Carbohydrate 42g (Dietary Fiber 0g); Protein 4g EXCHANGES: 1 Starch, 2 Other Carbohydrate, 2½ Fat CARBOHYDRATE CHOICES: 3

sweet note These brownies are very rich and ooey-gooey so be sure to serve with forks!

café coffee

Serving coffee? Let guests customize their cup by adding a splash of:

- Amaretto
- Hazelnut liqueur
- Kahlua
- Irish cream liqueur
- Raspberry-flavored liqueur
- Spiced rum

brownie ice cream cake

prep time: **25 minutes**   *start to finish:* **3 hours 55 minutes**   [16 SERVINGS]

1 box (1 lb 2.4 oz) Betty Crocker Original Supreme Premium brownie mix

Water, vegetable oil and egg called for on brownie mix box

½ gallon (8 cups) vanilla ice cream, slightly softened

1 cup hot fudge topping, warmed if desired

2 tablespoons candy sprinkles

16 red maraschino cherries with stems, drained

1 Heat oven to 350°F (325°F for dark or nonstick pans). Line 2 (9-inch) round cake pans with foil so foil extends about 2 inches over sides of pans; grease bottoms only with shortening or cooking spray.

2 Make brownie mix as directed on box, using pouch of chocolate syrup, water, oil and egg. Divide batter evenly between pans.

3 Bake 22 to 25 minutes or until toothpick inserted 2 inches from side of pan comes out almost clean. Cool completely in pans, about 1 hour. Do not remove from pans.

4 Spread slightly softened ice cream evenly on brownies in pans. Freeze at least 2 hours or until ice cream is firm.

5 Remove brownies from pan by lifting foil; peel foil from sides of brownies. Place on serving plates. Cut each dessert into 8 wedges. Drizzle each wedge with hot fudge topping. Decorate with candy sprinkles and cherries. Store covered in freezer.

1 SERVING: Calories 390; Total Fat 16g (Saturated Fat 7g; Trans Fat 0g); Cholesterol 55mg; Sodium 230mg; Total Carbohydrate 57g (Dietary Fiber 1g); Protein 5g EXCHANGES: 1 Starch, 3 Other Carbohydrate, 3 Fat CARBOHYDRATE CHOICES: 4

sweet note For a special gathering, set up a dessert bar with ice cream toppings and syrups. Add extras such as fresh strawberries, sliced bananas, chopped nuts and candies. Let guests build their own desserts.

brownie pops

prep time: **30 minutes**   *start to finish:* **2 hours 30 minutes**   [24 BROWNIE POPS]

1 box (1 lb 2.3 oz) Betty Crocker fudge brownie mix

Water, vegetable oil and eggs called for on brownie mix box

24 craft sticks (flat wooden sticks with round ends)

1 cup semisweet chocolate chips (6 oz)

2 teaspoons shortening

Assorted decors or sprinkles

1   Heat oven to 350°F. Line 13 × 9-inch pan with foil so foil extends about 2 inches over sides of pan. Spray foil with cooking spray.

2   Make brownie mix as directed on box, using water, oil and eggs. Spread in pan.

3   Bake as directed on box for 13 × 9-inch pan. Cool completely, about 1 hour.

4   Place brownies in freezer for 30 minutes. Remove brownies from pan by lifting foil; peel foil from sides of brownies. Cut brownies into 24 square bars, 6 rows by 4 rows. Gently insert stick into end of each bar, peeling foil from bars. Place on cookie sheet; freeze 30 minutes.

5   In microwavable bowl, microwave chocolate chips and shortening uncovered on High about 1 minute; stir until smooth. If necessary, microwave additional 5 seconds at a time. Dip top ⅓ to ½ of each brownie into chocolate; sprinkle with decors. Lay flat on waxed paper or foil to dry.

1 BROWNIE POP: Calories 150; Total Fat 6g (Saturated Fat 2g; Trans Fat 0g); Cholesterol 10mg; Sodium 80mg; Total Carbohydrate 24g (Dietary Fiber 0g); Protein 0g EXCHANGES: 1½ Other Carbohydrate, 1 Fat CARBOHYDRATE CHOICES: 1½

sweet note For a little different contrast, use white vanilla baking chips instead of the chocolate chips. Or, melt dark and white chocolate for variety. Look for a variety of candy sprinkles at a cake decorating supply store.

black forest brownie dessert

prep time: 20 minutes   *start to finish:* 1 hour 20 minutes   [6 SERVINGS]

1 pouch (10.25 oz) Betty Crocker fudge brownie mix

Water, vegetable oil and egg called for on the brownie mix pouch

1 can (21 oz) cherry pie filling

2 tablespoons amaretto, if desired

1 cup whipping cream

1 tablespoon powdered sugar

¼ teaspoon unsweetened baking cocoa, if desired

1 Heat oven to 350°F. Spray 9-inch glass pie plate with baking spray with flour.

2 Make brownies as directed on pouch, using water, oil and egg. Pour batter into pie plate.

3 Bake 24 to 26 minutes or until toothpick inserted in center comes out almost clean. Cool 30 minutes.

4 In small bowl, stir together pie filling and amaretto. Cut brownie into 6 wedges. Place each wedge on individual serving plate. Spoon about ⅓ cup cherry mixture over each wedge.

5 In medium bowl, beat whipping cream and powdered sugar with electric mixer on high speed until stiff peaks form. Add dollop of whipped cream to each serving. Sprinkle with cocoa.

1 SERVING: Calories 540; Total Fat 28g (Saturated Fat 10g; Trans Fat 1g); Cholesterol 80mg; Sodium 190mg; Total Carbohydrate 70g (Dietary Fiber 3g); Protein 4g EXCHANGES: 1 Starch, 3½ Other Carbohydrate, 5½ Fat CARBOHYDRATE CHOICES: 4½

sweet note Here's an easy version of the chocolate-cherry torte that originated in Germany's Black Forest region. The original torte uses kirsch, a cherry liqueur, instead of amaretto, and you could substitute cherry liqueur for the amaretto if you like.

fudgy brownie trifle

prep time: 15 minutes   *start to finish:* 6 hours 15 minutes   [20 SERVINGS]

1 box (1 lb 2.3 oz) Betty Crocker fudge brownie mix

Water, oil and eggs called for on brownie mix box

1 tablespoon instant coffee granules or crystals

1 box (4-serving size) chocolate fudge instant pudding and pie filling mix

2 cups cold milk

1 bag (10 oz) toffee bits

1 container (8 oz) frozen whipped topping, thawed

1   Heat oven to 350°F. Grease bottom only of 13 × 9-inch pan with shortening or cooking spray.

2   In medium bowl, stir brownie mix, water, oil and eggs until well blended. Stir coffee granules into batter. Spread in pan.

3   Bake 24 to 26 minutes or until toothpick inserted 2 inches from side of pan comes out almost clean. Cool completely, about 1 hour 30 minutes.

4   Cut brownies into 1-inch squares. In bottom of 3-quart glass bowl, place half of the brownie squares. Make pudding mix as directed on box for pudding, using milk. Pour half of the pudding over brownies in bowl. Top with half each of the toffee bits and whipped topping. Repeat with remaining brownies, pudding, toffee bits and whipped topping.

5   Cover; refrigerate at least 4 hours before serving. Store covered in refrigerator.

1 SERVING: Calories 270; Total Fat 11g (Saturated Fat 6g; Trans Fat 0g); Cholesterol 15mg; Sodium 190mg; Total Carbohydrate 40g (Dietary Fiber 1g); Protein 2g EXCHANGES: 1 Starch, 1½ Other Carbohydrate, 2 Fat CARBOHYDRATE CHOICES: 2½

sweet note Trifles are a traditional English dessert originally made with cake or ladyfingers covered with jam and custard, and topped with whipped cream. This recipe is a rich chocolaty version with a mild coffee flavor. There's no fruit in this trifle but you can garnish with fresh strawberries (dipped in chocolate if you like) or raspberries for a pretty finish.

brownies and chocolate-raspberry fondue

prep time: **20 minutes** *start to finish:* **2 hours** [16 SERVINGS]

1 box (1 lb 2.4 oz) Betty Crocker Original Supreme Premium brownie mix

Water, vegetable oil and egg called for on brownie mix box

1 container (1 lb) chocolate creamy ready-to-spread frosting

⅓ cup seedless raspberry preserves

Assorted fresh fruit (orange sections, whole strawberries, banana slices and raspberries) and marshmallows, as desired

1 Heat oven to 350°F (325°F for dark or nonstick pan). Grease bottom only of 8- or 9-inch square pan with shortening or cooking spray.

2 Make brownie mix as directed on box, using pouch of chocolate syrup, water, oil and egg. Spread batter in pan.

3 Bake as directed on box for 8- or 9-inch pan. Cool completely, about 1 hour.

4 In microwavable bowl, stir frosting and preserves. Microwave uncovered on High about 20 seconds or until mixture can be stirred smooth. Pour into fondue pot. Keep warm over low heat, and serve within 1 hour.

5 Cut brownies into squares. Spear brownies and fruit with fondue forks; dip in fondue.

1 SERVING : Calories 280; Total Fat 9g (Saturated Fat 2g; Trans Fat 1.5g); Cholesterol 15mg; Sodium 190mg; Total Carbohydrate 49g (Dietary Fiber 0g); Protein 1g EXCHANGES: ½ Starch, 2½ Other Carbohydrate, 2 Fat CARBOHYDRATE CHOICES: 3

sweet note For easier removal of the brownies, line the baking pan with foil. Then after baking, lift out the cooled brownies for easy cutting.

turtle tart

prep time: **25 minutes**   *start to finish:* **3 hours 15 minutes**   [16 SERVINGS]

cookie base

1 pouch (1 lb 1.5 oz) Betty Crocker oatmeal cookie mix

½ cup butter or margarine, softened

1 tablespoon water

1 egg

1 cup chopped pecans

filling

40 caramels, unwrapped

⅓ cup whipping cream

¾ cup chopped pecans

topping

1 bag (11.5 oz) milk chocolate chips (2 cups)

⅓ cup whipping cream

¼ cup chopped pecans

1 Heat oven to 350°F.

2 In large bowl, stir cookie mix, butter, water and egg until soft dough forms. Stir in 1 cup pecans. In ungreased 9-inch tart pan with removable bottom, press dough in bottom and up side.

3 Bake 19 to 21 minutes or until light golden brown. Cool 10 minutes.

4 Meanwhile, in medium microwavable bowl, microwave caramels and ⅓ cup whipping cream uncovered on High 2 to 4 minutes, stirring twice, until caramels are melted. Stir in ¾ cup pecans. Spread over cooled crust. Refrigerate 15 minutes.

5 In another medium microwavable bowl, microwave chocolate chips and ⅓ cup whipping cream uncovered on High 1 to 2 minutes, stirring every 30 seconds, until chocolate is smooth. Pour over filling. Sprinkle with ¼ cup pecans. Refrigerate 2 hours or until set.

6 To serve, let stand at room temperature 10 minutes before cutting. Store covered in refrigerator.

1 SERVING: Calories 520; Total Fat 29g (Saturated Fat 10g; Trans Fat 0g); Cholesterol 45mg; Sodium 240mg; Total Carbohydrate 59g (Dietary Fiber 3g); Protein 7g EXCHANGES: ½ Starch, 3½ Other Carbohydrate, ½ High-Fat Meat, 5 Fat CARBOHYDRATE CHOICES: 4

sweet note If you don't have a tart pan, just use a 13 × 9-inch pan, and cut into squares instead of wedges.

almond cheesecake

prep time: 40 minutes   *start to finish:* 7 hours 45 minutes   [16 SERVINGS]

crust

1 box (1 lb 2.25 oz) Betty Crocker SuperMoist yellow cake mix

½ cup butter or margarine, softened

filling

3 packages (8 oz each) cream cheese, softened

¾ cup sugar

1 cup whipping cream

1 teaspoon almond extract

3 eggs

garnish

¼ cup sliced almonds

4 teaspoons sugar

Fresh raspberries, if desired

sweet note This lovely, rich cheesecake is ideal for a party. Remove the side of the pan, then slide onto a large serving platter. Surround the cheesecake with more fresh raspberries and edible flowers for a fancy presentation.

1   Heat oven to 350°F (325°F for dark or nonstick pan). Spray bottom and side of 10-inch springform pan with baking spray with flour. Wrap outside of pan with foil.

2   Reserve ½ cup of the cake mix; set aside. In large bowl, beat remaining cake mix and butter with electric mixer on low speed until crumbly. Press in bottom and 1½ inches up side of pan.

3   Bake 15 minutes or until edges are golden brown. Reduce oven temperature to 325°F (300°F for dark or nonstick pan).

4   In same large bowl, beat reserved ½ cup cake mix and cream cheese on medium speed until well blended. Beat in ¾ cup sugar, the whipping cream and almond extract on medium speed until smooth and creamy. On low speed, beat in eggs, one at a time, until well blended. Pour batter over crust. Place springform pan in large roasting pan; place on oven rack. Pour enough boiling water into roasting pan to cover half of side of springform pan.

5   Bake 55 to 60 minutes or until edge is set but center jiggles slightly when moved. Cool in pan (in water bath) on cooling rack 20 minutes. Remove pan from water bath. Carefully run knife around side of pan to loosen, but do not remove side of pan. Cool 1 hour 30 minutes at room temperature. Cover loosely; refrigerate at least 4 hours or overnight.

6   In 1-quart saucepan, cook almonds and 4 teaspoons sugar over low heat about 10 minutes, stirring constantly, until sugar is melted and almonds are coated. Cool on waxed paper; break apart.

7   Remove side of pan before serving. Garnish cheesecake with sugared almonds and raspberries. Store covered in refrigerator.

1 SERVING: Calories 440; Total Fat 30g (Saturated Fat 17g; Trans Fat 1.5g); Cholesterol 120mg; Sodium 390mg; Total Carbohydrate 39g (Dietary Fiber 0g); Protein 6g EXCHANGES: 1 Starch, 1½ Other Carbohydrate, ½ High-Fat Meat, 5 Fat CARBOHYDRATE CHOICES: 2½

impossibly easy toffee bar cheesecake

prep time: 10 minutes   *start to finish:* 5 hours 45 minutes   [8 SERVINGS]

¼ cup milk

2 teaspoons vanilla

2 eggs

¾ cup packed brown sugar

¼ cup Original Bisquick mix

2 packages (8 oz each) cream cheese, cut into 16 pieces, softened

3 bars (1.4 oz each) chocolate-covered English toffee candy, coarsely chopped

½ cup caramel topping

1 Heat oven to 325°F. Spray bottom of 9-inch glass pie plate with cooking spray.

2 In blender, place milk, vanilla, eggs, brown sugar and Bisquick mix. Cover; blend on high speed 15 seconds. Add cream cheese. Cover; blend 2 minutes. Pour into pie plate.

3 Sprinkle candy over top; swirl gently with table knife to evenly distribute candy.

4 Bake 30 to 35 minutes or until about 2 inches of edge of pie is set and center is still soft and jiggles slightly when moved. Cool completely, about 1 hour.

5 Refrigerate at least 4 hours. Serve with caramel topping. Store covered in refrigerator.

1 SERVING: Calories 460; Total Fat 27g (Saturated Fat 16g; Trans Fat 1g); Cholesterol 125mg; Sodium 360mg; Total Carbohydrate 47g (Dietary Fiber 0g); Protein 7g EXCHANGES: 3 Other Carbohydrate, 1 High-Fat Meat, 4 Fat CARBOHYDRATE CHOICES: 3

sweet note You can also serve this creamy cheesecake with chocolate topping instead of the caramel.

rainbow sherbet roll

prep time: **15 minutes**   *start to finish:* **9 hours 25 minutes**   [12 SERVINGS]

1 box (1 lb) Betty Crocker white angel food cake mix

1¼ cups cold water

Powdered sugar

1½ cups raspberry sherbet, softened

1½ cups orange sherbet, softened

1½ cups lime sherbet, softened

1 Preheat oven to 350°F. Line 15 × 10 × 1-inch jelly roll pan with waxed paper.

2 In extra-large glass or metal bowl, beat cake mix and cold water with electric mixer on low speed 30 seconds. Beat on medium speed 1 minute. Spread half of the batter in pan. Spread remaining batter in ungreased 9 × 5-inch loaf pan.

3 Bake jelly roll pan 20 to 25 minutes, loaf pan 35 to 45 minutes, or until top springs back when lightly touched in center. Reserve loaf pan for another use. Cool jelly roll pan 10 minutes. Loosen cake from edges of pan; turn upside down onto towel sprinkled with powdered sugar. Carefully remove waxed paper. Trim off stiff edges of cake if necessary. Carefully roll hot cake and towel from narrow end. Cool completely on cooling rack, about 1 hour.

4 Unroll cake; remove towel. Beginning at a narrow end, spread raspberry sherbet on ⅓ of cake, orange sherbet on next third of cake and lime sherbet on remaining cake. Roll up carefully. Place roll, seam side down, on 18 × 12-inch piece of foil. Wrap in foil; freeze at least 6 hours until firm.

5 Remove from freezer 15 minutes before serving. Cut roll into ¾-inch slices. Store wrapped in freezer.

sweet note Rolling the cake is easy if you have the right towel. Use a clean, low-lint cotton kitchen towel with a tight broadcloth or flour-sack weave.

1 SERVING: Calories 230; Total Fat 1g (Saturated Fat 0.5g; Trans Fat 0g); Cholesterol 0mg; Sodium 350mg; Total Carbohydrate 51g (Dietary Fiber 0g); Protein 3g EXCHANGES: 1 Starch, 2½ Other Carbohydrate CARBOHYDRATE CHOICES: 3½

pumpkin dessert squares

prep time: **15 minutes**   *start to finish:* **1 hour 40 minutes**   [15 SERVINGS]

base

1½ cups Original Bisquick mix

½ cup cold butter or margarine

½ cup chopped pecans

filling

1 cup granulated sugar

1 can (15 oz) pumpkin (not pumpkin pie mix)

1 can (12 oz) evaporated milk

4 teaspoons pumpkin pie spice

3 eggs

topping

1 cup Original Bisquick mix

½ cup packed brown sugar

¼ cup cold butter or margarine

¾ cup chopped pecans

sweet note Make this when you want to serve pumpkin pie but need to serve a crowd. Because it makes 15 servings, it's an ideal and delicious alternative!

1 Heat oven to 350F. Spray bottom only of 13 × 9-inch pan with cooking spray.

2 In medium bowl, mix 1½ cups Bisquick mix and ½ cup pecans. Using pastry blender or fork, cut in ½ cup butter until mixture is crumbly. With floured fingers, press mixture in bottom of pan. Bake 10 minutes.

3 Meanwhile, in large bowl, beat filling ingredients with whisk until smooth; set aside. In medium bowl, mix 1 cup Bisquick mix and ½ cup brown sugar. Using pastry blender or fork, cut in ¼ cup butter until mixture is crumbly. Stir in pecans. Pour filling over hot partially baked base. Sprinkle topping over filling.

4 Bake 50 to 55 minutes or until toothpick inserted in center comes out clean. Cool 30 minutes before cutting into squares. Serve with whipped cream, if desired. Store in refrigerator.

1 SERVING: Calories 370; Total Fat 21g (Saturated Fat 9g; Trans Fat 1g); Cholesterol 75mg; Sodium 350mg; Total Carbohydrate 40g (Dietary Fiber 2g); Protein 5g EXCHANGES: 1½ Starch, 1 Other Carbohydrate, 4 Fat CARBOHYDRATE CHOICES: 2½

dollop away!

To add a special touch to any dessert, make your own whipped cream to dollop on top. Beat ¼ cup whipping cream and 1½ teaspoons granulated or powdered sugar with an electric mixer on high speed until soft peaks form. The cream will whip faster if you chill the bowl and beaters in the freezer for about 15 minutes before whipping.

impossibly easy banana custard pie

prep time: **15 minutes**   *start to finish:* **4 hours**   [8 SERVINGS]

1 cup mashed ripe bananas (2 medium)

2 teaspoons lemon juice

½ cup Original Bisquick mix

¼ cup sugar

1 tablespoon butter or margarine, softened

½ teaspoon vanilla

2 eggs

1 can (14 oz) sweetened condensed milk (not evaporated)

¾ cup frozen (thawed) whipped topping

¼ cup coarsely chopped walnuts, if desired

Caramel topping, warmed, if desired

1 Heat oven to 350°F. Spray 9-inch glass pie plate with cooking spray.

2 In small bowl, mix bananas and lemon juice; set aside.

3 In medium bowl, stir remaining ingredients except whipped topping, walnuts and caramel topping until blended. Add banana mixture; stir until blended. Pour into pie plate.

4 Bake 40 to 45 minutes or until golden brown and knife inserted in center comes out clean. Cool at room temperature 1 hour.

5 Cover; refrigerate about 2 hours or until chilled. Spread with whipped topping; sprinkle with walnuts. Drizzle with caramel topping. Store covered in refrigerator.

1 SERVING: Calories 300; Total Fat 10g (Saturated Fat 5g; Trans Fat 0g); Cholesterol 75mg; Sodium 180mg; Total Carbohydrate 47g (Dietary Fiber 1g); Protein 6g EXCHANGES: ½ Starch, 2½ Other Carbohydrate, ½ High-Fat Meat, 1 Fat CARBOHYDRATE CHOICES: 3

sweet note Don't throw away those speckled brown bananas! Their sweet ripe flavor and soft texture are what make this easy pie so delicious.

bonus chapter

gluten-free desserts

brownie ganache torte with raspberries

prep time: **15 minutes**   *start to finish:* **1 hour 55 minutes**   [12 SERVINGS]

1 box (16 oz) Betty Crocker Gluten Free brownie mix

¼ cup butter, melted

2 eggs

⅓ cup whipping cream

½ cup semisweet chocolate chips

1 cup fresh raspberries or sliced strawberries

1 Heat oven to 350°F (325°F for dark or nonstick pan). Spray bottom only of 8-inch springform pan with cooking spray.

2 In medium bowl, stir brownie mix, butter and eggs until well blended. Spread in pan.

3 Bake 26 to 29 minutes or until toothpick inserted 2 inches from side of pan comes out almost clean; cool 10 minutes. Run knife around edge of pan to loosen; remove side of pan. Cool completely, about 1 hour.

4 In 1-quart saucepan, heat whipping cream over medium-low heat until hot. Remove from heat; stir in chocolate chips until melted and smooth. Let stand 15 minutes to thicken.

5 Carefully pour chocolate mixture onto top center of brownie; spread just to edge. Top with raspberries. Cut into wedges.

1 SERVING: Calories 270; Total Fat 11g (Saturated Fat 7g; Trans Fat 0g); Cholesterol 55mg; Sodium 110mg; Total Carbohydrate 38g (Dietary Fiber 1g); Protein 2g EXCHANGES: 1 Starch, 1½ Other Carbohydrate, 2 Fat CARBOHYDRATE CHOICES: 2½

sweet note In addition to the fresh raspberries, top these fudgy wedges with a dollop of whipped cream and a few toasted slivered almonds. Spectacular!

pumpkin–chocolate chip cookies

prep time: **30 minutes**   *start to finish:* **1 hour**   [3 DOZEN COOKIES]

¾ cup canned pumpkin (not pumpkin pie mix)

¼ cup butter, softened (not melted)

1 teaspoon gluten-free vanilla

1 egg

1 box (19 oz) Betty Crocker Gluten Free chocolate chip cookie mix

½ cup raisins, if desired

¼ teaspoon ground cinnamon

Powdered sugar, if desired

1 Heat oven to 350°F (325°F for dark or nonstick pans). Grease cookie sheets with shortening.

2 In large bowl, stir pumpkin, butter, vanilla and egg until blended. Stir in cookie mix, raisins and cinnamon until soft dough forms. Drop dough by rounded tablespoonfuls 2 inches apart on cookie sheet.

3 Bake 10 to 12 minutes or until almost no indentation remains when lightly touched in center and edges are golden brown. Immediately remove from cookie sheet to cooling rack. Cool completely, about 15 minutes. Sprinkle with powdered sugar.

1 COOKIE: Calories 80; Total Fat 2.5g (Saturated Fat 1.5g; Trans Fat 0g); Cholesterol 10mg; Sodium 80mg; Total Carbohydrate 13g (Dietary Fiber 0g); Protein 0g EXCHANGES: 1 Other Carbohydrate, ½ Fat CARBOHYDRATE CHOICES: 1

check the label

Always read labels to make sure each recipe ingredient that you are using is gluten free. Products and ingredient sources can change. Look for the Betty Crocker gluten-free mixes used in these recipes with the other baking products at the grocery store.

sweet note Dried currants or cranberries are easy choices that can be substituted for the raisins.

cookie-brownie bars

prep time: 20 minutes   *start to finish:* 1 hour 55 minutes   [24 BARS]

cookie

1 box (19 oz) Betty Crocker Gluten Free chocolate chip cookie mix

½ cup butter, softened

1 teaspoon gluten-free vanilla

1 egg

brownie

1 box (16 oz) Betty Crocker Gluten Free brownie mix

¼ cup butter, melted

2 eggs

1 Heat oven to 350°F (325°F for dark or nonstick pan). Grease bottom only of 13 × 9-inch pan with shortening or cooking spray.

2 In medium bowl, stir cookie ingredients until soft dough forms. Drop dough by rounded tablespoonfuls onto bottom of pan.

3 In another medium bowl, stir brownie ingredients until well blended. Drop batter by tablespoonfuls evenly between mounds of cookie dough.

4 Bake 30 to 35 minutes or until cookie portion is golden brown. Cool completely, about 1 hour. For bars, cut into 6 rows by 4 rows.

1 BAR: Calories 180; Total Fat 7g (Saturated Fat 4g; Trans Fat 0g); Cholesterol 30mg; Sodium 140mg; Total Carbohydrate 26g (Dietary Fiber 0g); Protein 1g EXCHANGES: ½ Starch, 1 Other Carbohydrate, 1½ Fat CARBOHYDRATE CHOICES: 2

sweet note Arrange these double-delicious bars on a pretty platter for serving. No one will guess that they are indeed gluten free!

lemon lover's cupcakes
with lemon buttercream frosting

prep time: **20 minutes**   *start to finish:* **1 hour 25 minutes**   [12 CUPCAKES]

cupcakes

1 box (15 oz) Betty Crocker Gluten Free yellow cake mix

⅔ cup water

½ cup butter, melted

3 eggs, beaten

2 tablespoons grated lemon peel

frosting

2 cups powdered sugar

¼ cup butter, softened

1 teaspoon grated lemon peel

2 to 3 tablespoons fresh lemon juice

1 Heat oven to 350°F (325°F for dark or nonstick pan). Place paper baking cup in each of 12 regular-size muffin cups.

2 In large bowl, stir cake mix, water, melted butter, eggs and 2 tablespoons lemon peel just until dry ingredients are moistened. Divide batter evenly among muffin cups (about ⅔ full).

3 Bake 18 to 23 minutes or until toothpick inserted in center comes out clean. Cool 10 minutes; remove from pan to cooling rack. Cool completely, about 30 minutes.

4 In medium bowl, beat powdered sugar, softened butter and 1 tablespoon of the lemon juice with electric mixer on low speed until mixed. Add remaining lemon juice, 1 teaspoon at a time, until creamy and smooth. Beat in 1 teaspoon lemon peel. Frost cupcakes.

1 CUPCAKE: Calories 330; Total Fat 13g (Saturated Fat 8g; Trans Fat 0g); Cholesterol 85mg; Sodium 290mg; Total Carbohydrate 51g (Dietary Fiber 0g); Protein 2g EXCHANGES: ½ Starch, 3 Other Carbohydrate, 2½ Fat CARBOHYDRATE CHOICES: 3½

sweet note Grate only the bright yellow portion of the lemon peel for the best flavor. The "pith," or white part of the skin, is bitter.

banana cupcakes with browned butter frosting

prep time: **20 minutes**   *start to finish:* **1 hour 25 minutes**   [17 CUPCAKES]

cupcakes

1 box (15 oz) Betty Crocker Gluten Free yellow cake mix

1 cup mashed ripe bananas (2 medium)

⅓ cup butter, melted*

⅓ cup water

3 eggs, beaten

2 teaspoons gluten-free vanilla

frosting and garnish

⅓ cup butter*

3 cups powdered sugar

1 teaspoon gluten-free vanilla

3 to 4 tablespoons milk

Banana slices, if desired

1 Heat oven to 350°F (325°F for dark or nonstick pans). Place paper baking cups in each of 17 regular-size muffin cups.

2 In large bowl, stir cupcake ingredients just until dry ingredients are moistened. Divide batter evenly among muffin cups (about ⅔ full).

3 Bake 16 to 18 minutes or until toothpick inserted in center comes out clean. Cool 10 minutes; remove from pan to cooling rack. Cool completely, about 30 minutes.

4 In 1-quart saucepan, heat ⅓ cup butter over medium heat just until light brown, stirring occasionally. (Watch carefully because butter can burn quickly.) Remove from heat. Cool slightly, about 5 minutes.

5 In medium bowl, beat browned butter, powdered sugar, vanilla and enough milk until frosting is smooth and spreadable. Frost cupcakes. Top each cupcake with a banana slice.

Do not use margarine or vegetable oil spreads.

1 CUPCAKE: Calories 270; Total Fat 8g (Saturated Fat 5g; Trans Fat 0g); Cholesterol 55mg; Sodium 200mg; Total Carbohydrate 46g (Dietary Fiber 0g); Protein 2g EXCHANGES: ½ Starch, 2½ Other Carbohydrate, 1½ Fat CARBOHYDRATE CHOICES: 3

sweet note "Browned butter," made by heating the butter until it becomes light hazelnut in color, adds a wonderful, unforgettable flavor that has no equal or substitution.

carrot cake

prep time: **15 minutes**   *start to finish:* **1 hour 55 minutes**   [12 SERVINGS]

cake

1 box (15 oz) Betty Crocker Gluten Free yellow cake mix

⅔ cup water

½ cup butter, softened

½ teaspoon ground cinnamon

¼ teaspoon ground nutmeg

2 teaspoons gluten-free vanilla

3 eggs

1 cup finely shredded carrots (2 medium)

¼ cup finely chopped pecans or walnuts

frosting

4 oz (half of 8-oz package) cream cheese, softened

2 tablespoons butter

½ teaspoon gluten-free vanilla

1 to 3 teaspoons milk

2 cups powdered sugar

¼ cup flaked coconut, toasted if desired*

sweet note Finely shredding the carrot and finely chopping the nuts spreads their flavor through the whole cake and makes the cake easier to cut, too.

1 Heat oven to 350°F (325°F for dark or nonstick pan). Grease bottom only of 8- or 9-inch square pan with shortening or cooking spray.

2 In large bowl, beat cake mix, water, ½ cup butter, the cinnamon, nutmeg, 2 teaspoons vanilla and eggs on low speed 30 seconds. Beat on medium speed 2 minutes, scraping bowl occasionally. With spoon, stir in carrots and pecans. Spread in pan.

3 Bake 36 to 41 minutes for 8-inch pan or 33 to 38 minutes for 9-inch pan or until toothpick inserted in center comes out clean. Cool completely, about 1 hour.

4 In large bowl, beat cream cheese, 2 tablespoons butter, ½ teaspoon vanilla and 1 teaspoon milk with electric mixer on low speed until smooth. Gradually beat in powdered sugar, 1 cup at a time, until smooth and spreadable. If frosting is too thick, beat in more milk, a few drops at a time. Frost cake. Sprinkle with coconut.

*To toast coconut, spread in ungreased shallow pan. Bake uncovered at 350°F for 5 to 7 minutes, stirring occasionally, until golden brown.

1 SERVING: Calories 420; Total Fat 16g (Saturated Fat 9g; Trans Fat 0g); Cholesterol 90mg; Sodium 310mg; Total Carbohydrate 66g (Dietary Fiber 0g); Protein 3g EXCHANGES: 1 Starch, 3½ Other Carbohydrate, 3 Fat CARBOHYDRATE CHOICES: 4½

fresh baked is best

Baked goods made from gluten-free ingredients and Betty Crocker mixes will taste best when eaten the day they are baked. However, these products freeze well. Wrap small amounts in airtight containers. When you're ready to serve, thaw only what you need.

marble cake

prep time: **20 minutes**   *start to finish:* **2 hours 20 minutes**   [16 SERVINGS]

yellow cake

1 box (15 oz) Betty Crocker Gluten Free yellow cake mix

½ cup butter, softened

⅔ cup water

2 teaspoons gluten-free vanilla

3 eggs

devil's food cake

1 box (15 oz) Betty Crocker Gluten Free devil's food cake mix

½ cup butter, softened

1 cup water

3 eggs

frosting

3 cups powdered sugar

⅓ cup butter, softened

2 teaspoons gluten-free vanilla

3 oz unsweetened baking chocolate, melted, cooled

3 to 4 tablespoons milk

1 Heat oven to 350°F (325°F for dark or nonstick pans). Grease bottoms only of 2 (8- or 9-inch) round cake pans with shortening or cooking spray.

2 In large bowl, beat yellow cake ingredients with electric mixer on low speed 30 seconds. Beat on medium speed 2 minutes, scraping bowl occasionally; set aside. In another large bowl, beat devil's food cake ingredients on low speed 30 seconds. Beat on medium speed 2 minutes, scraping bowl occasionally.

3 Spoon yellow and devil's food batters alternately into pans, dividing evenly. Cut through batters with table knife in zigzag pattern for marbled design.

4 Bake 40 to 45 minutes or until toothpick inserted in center comes out clean. Cool 15 minutes; remove from pans to cooling racks. Cool completely, top sides up, about 1 hour.

5 In medium bowl, beat powdered sugar and ⅓ cup butter with spoon or electric mixer on low speed until blended. Stir in 2 teaspoons vanilla and the chocolate. Gradually beat in just enough milk to make frosting smooth and spreadable.

6 On serving plate, place 1 cake, rounded side down (trim rounded side if necessary so cake rests flat). Spread with ¼ cup frosting. Top with second cake, rounded side up. Frost side and top of cake with remaining frosting.

1 SERVING: Calories 490; Total Fat 21g (Saturated Fat 12g; Trans Fat 0.5g); Cholesterol 120mg; Sodium 430mg; Total Carbohydrate 70g (Dietary Fiber 1g); Protein 4g EXCHANGES: 1½ Starch, 3 Other Carbohydrate, 4 Fat CARBOHYDRATE CHOICES: 4½

sweet note Because of the way these special mixes are designed, butter is recommended for the success of this recipe.

metric conversion guide

volume

U.S. UNITS	CANADIAN METRIC	AUSTRALIAN METRIC
¼ teaspoon	1 mL	1 ml
½ teaspoon	2 mL	2 ml
1 teaspoon	5 mL	5 ml
1 tablespoon	15 mL	20 ml
¼ cup	50 mL	60 ml
⅓ cup	75 mL	80 ml
½ cup	125 mL	125 ml
⅔ cup	150 mL	170 ml
¾ cup	175 mL	190 ml
1 cup	250 mL	250 ml
1 quart	1 liter	1 liter
1½ quarts	1.5 liters	1.5 liters
2 quarts	2 liters	2 liters
2½ quarts	2.5 liters	2.5 liters
3 quarts	3 liters	3 liters
4 quarts	4 liters	4 liters

measurements

INCHES	CENTIMETERS
1	2.5
2	5.0
3	7.5
4	10.0
5	12.5
6	15.0
7	17.5
8	20.5
9	23.0
10	25.5
11	28.0
12	30.5
13	33.0

weight

U.S. UNITS	CANADIAN METRIC	AUSTRALIAN METRIC
1 ounce	30 grams	30 grams
2 ounces	55 grams	60 grams
3 ounces	85 grams	90 grams
4 ounces (¼ pound)	115 grams	125 grams
8 ounces (½ pound)	225 grams	225 grams
16 ounces (1 pound)	455 grams	500 grams
1 pound	455 grams	0.5 kilogram

temperatures

FAHRENHEIT	CELSIUS
32°	0°
212°	100°
250°	120°
275°	140°
300°	150°
325°	160°
350°	180°
375°	190°
400°	200°
425°	220°
450°	230°
475°	240°
500°	260°

note: The recipes in this cookbook have not been developed or tested using metric measures. When converting recipes to metric, some variations in quality may be noted.

recipes by mix

cookie mix

original bisquick mix and bisquick heart smart mix

Get started today and save on these Betty Crocker® products

Get started today and save on these Betty Crocker® products